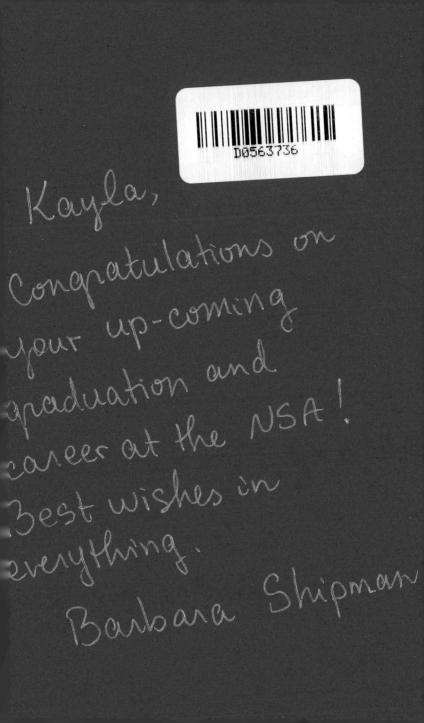

Kayla,

Congratulations on
your up-coming
graduation and
career at the NSA!
Best wishes in
everything.

Barbara Shipman

THE
LITTLE
ORANGE
BOOK

THE LITTLE ORANGE BOOK

SHORT LESSONS IN
EXCELLENT TEACHING

THE UNIVERSITY OF TEXAS SYSTEM
Academy of Distinguished Teachers

cooperation innovation assessment engagement collaboration
creativity mentorship technique development sharing skills
daring foresight growth learning technology communication

DISTRIBUTED BY TOWER BOOKS
AN IMPRINT OF THE UNIVERSITY OF TEXAS PRESS

Requests for permission to reproduce material from this work should
be sent to:

    Permissions
    University of Texas Press
    P.O. Box 7819
    Austin, TX 78713-7819
    utpress.utexas.edu/rp-form

♾ The paper used in this book meets the minimum requirements of
ANSI/NISO Z39.48-1992 (R1997) (Permanence of Paper).

LIBRARY OF CONGRESS CATALOGING-IN-PUBLICATION DATA
The little orange book : short lessons in excellent teaching / The
University of Texas System, Academy of Distinguished Teachers. —
First edition.
    pages cm
  ISBN 978-1-4773-0235-4 (cloth : alk. paper)
  1. Teaching.   I. University of Texas System. Academy of
Distinguished Teachers.
  LB1025.3.I57   2015
  371.102—dc23

                              2014046086

CONTENTS

TEACHING AND LEARNING
IS BASED ON COMMUNICATION

COLLEGE STUDENTS NEED
TO LEARN HOW TO LEARN

INTRODUCTION

TEACHING IS A POWERFUL profession. Whether you teach workshop-style classes of twenty-five students or convene your class in lecture halls with five hundred or more students, whether you teach first-year students or doctoral ones, your influence is profound. You are the representative of and the gateway into your discipline, and it is up to you to ensure students learn what they need to know to move on to the next level. But more than that, you have the potential to change students' lives—to encourage them to think openly and strategically about the world around them, to help them communicate effectively with a wide range of audiences, and to help them contribute to the disciplinary, public, and personal communities to which they currently belong and the ones to which they aspire to belong someday.

But that potential, that power, that responsibility can be overshadowed by day-to-day uncertainties about how to be an effective teacher. Where can you turn to get advice or practical suggestions from experts? *The Little Orange Book: Short Lessons in Excellent Teaching* is modeled after *Harvey Penick's Little Red Book: Lessons and Teachings from a Lifetime in Golf.* The vignettes included here were written by the sixteen members of the University of Texas System Academy of Distinguished Teachers. This honorific group represents the most accomplished and renowned teachers from the entire University of Texas System. The UT System has nine academic campuses and over 200,000 students. Each campus has some shade of orange as its chosen school color, inspiring the title of this volume, but the pieces are intended to be relevant well beyond the Lone Star State.

The Little Orange Book contains short essays focused on the practical fundamentals of great teaching, revealing best strategies in and out of the classroom, no matter what the discipline or level of instruction. The topics range from simple but important tips such as remembering students' names and creating a safe zone within the classroom to more advanced considerations such as determining when to use groups and drawing concepts for better understanding. There are also motivational pieces that focus on inspiring curiosity and introducing students to the tantalizing secrets of your discipline. Intermixed with the passages are one-liners and questions intended to provoke thought, reflection, discussion, and, ultimately, inspiration to try new things in your own class.

We hope that readers—new and experienced teachers alike—will find many useful suggestions while reading *The Little Orange Book*. Teaching at all levels is currently undergoing tremendous change, and it will continue to do so. But the fundamentals of great teaching, like the fundamentals of a great golf game, are timeless.

BETH BRUNK-CHAVEZ AND BRENT IVERSON

EVERYONE IS A TEACHER

MUCH LIKE RINGS signifying the age and life of a tree, the number of titles that we acquire increases over time and reflects our life paths. For example, the first title that we all get is son or daughter, perhaps brother or sister, too. We then become students, writers, golfers, dancers, cooks, girl scouts, drivers, graduates, fathers, and so on. One could argue that the definition of a full life includes the number of titles we collect along the way. One title of particular significance, however, is *teacher*. Whether or not we embrace the role, we are all teachers. Some do it well and some don't, but we all will be teaching others at various points in our lives.

The notion that everyone is a teacher, in fact, should be embraced, because the ability to

> The notion that everyone is a teacher, in fact, should be embraced, because the ability to teach anything connects to the ability to learn what is being taught.

teach anything connects to the ability to learn what is being taught. The sooner students recognize that teaching others—a noble act of service—also greatly benefits them, the sooner they will become deep learners. Consider the simple act of reading an article in the daily newspaper.

As we read, we gain information. But what if we read the same article with the requirement that later we must explain it to someone else? Would we read the article differently? Undoubtedly, the answer is yes, because the need to explain (or teach) would cause us to read for deeper understanding as well as to develop connections within the article and to our existing knowledge base to use in our explanations. The power of the explanation requires a more refined understanding of the article. The article contains information; the explanation demonstrates knowledge.

Savvy students put themselves in positions to explain content, whether that means teaching another person informally outside of class or delivering a mock lecture to a hypothetical class in their apartment or dorm room. Savvy instructors recognize the value that teaching within peer groups provides, and they create obvious formal or informal mechanisms to promote this type of learning in their classrooms.

Of course, the title *teacher* does not require connection to an official class. The simple sharing of talents or expertise is the very definition of teaching. It is the noblest of acts, as a teacher invests time in someone else, raising that person to a higher level. We should encourage all, especially young students, to share their passions with others. It might become a habit. If you play the piano, ask roommates, friends, or just anyone who will listen, to sit next to you, and teach them to play a few notes. If you dance, bring that experience to others. If you cook, then encourage others to cook with you. Your passion and expertise will draw them in, for mutual benefit. And it will undoubtedly be fun or, at the very least, interesting. What kind of campus environment would a university have—in fact, what kind of world would we experience—if we all invested in each other through the sharing of our knowledge and passions? It would be a true community of scholarship, in which learning is a shared endeavor among peers.

In short, if we want to become better at something, we should teach it to others. Everyone is a teacher. We should run toward that worthy title for the benefit of everyone, including ourselves.

JOHN SIBERT

How do you know your students are learning?

IT STARTS WITH ATTITUDE

HARD ON STANDARDS,
SOFT ON STUDENTS

I BELIEVE IN STANDARDS, challenging requirements, consistency of application, and academic rigor. I believe in holding myself to the same standards of evidence and proof to which I hold my students, practicing what I advocate for the students, and honestly admitting discrepancies in my own thought and action. All of these are essential for academic rigor as well as for intellectual integrity in teaching.

I also believe students should be intellectually challenged and encouraged to achieve everything they are capable of, even if they aren't totally supportive of this encouragement. Most students have never been pushed to actualize their academic potential, and I believe it is our job as professors to press for that to happen. But I also believe that while we are being hard on standards, we must also be engaged in empathy, compassion, and nurturing.

Many students (and not just first-generation students) need to be psychologically nurtured to make it through any one course, not to mention an entire academic degree. Experiencing empathy in an academic environment may help them make the attitudinal adjustments necessary to continue their education. How can both ends of this values spectrum come together in your classroom? My way of integrating them into instruction is to be hard on the standards but soft on the students. Here's how that would look. If a student asks that his late assignment not lose points (the consequence of losing points for turning the assignment in late was on the syllabus), a required project be forgiven, a grade be improperly changed, or an inappropriate exception be made, I can express empathy by communicating that I understand why what he is requesting is desirable and important to him. I can also explain that standards and rules are meant to be followed, and that, in the spirit of fairness, professors can't make individual exceptions for one student without making the same exceptions for the rest of the students. A typical response might be: "I can understand how disappointed you are to lose points on this late assignment, and I'm hoping that it will be here on time next week. Meanwhile, let me know if you have any other questions that I can help you with. It is very important to me that you succeed."

Academic standards (mine, the department's, or the system's) are to be respected and upheld. But students deserve our emotional support and nurturing as they make progress adapting to those rules and expectations and "getting with the academic program" necessary for them to graduate.

An outside benefit of this hard-on-standards-but-soft-on-students policy is that students may be less likely to take out their resentment over unpopular rules on the professor. They may be less likely to kill a caring messenger or to retaliate on course evaluations or social media.

> Empathy is not agreeing that a standard or rule is right or wrong (that's not the issue); it is instead communicating that you care about the student and her feelings about the rule and the impact she believes the rule is having on her life.

Let me be clear. Empathy is not agreeing that a standard or rule is right or wrong (that's not the issue); it is instead communicating that you care about the student and her feelings about the rule and the impact she believes the rule is having on her life. Empathy is neither sympathy nor agreement, and it is not taking sides about the rules. It is temporarily leaving your role as a professor who must make judgments as a legitimate part of the job and trying to see your course or the university through the student's eyes. It is nurturing the student without compromising academic rigor. I believe our university students need both in order to succeed.

MARY LYNN CROW

It is the intrinsic rewards
to good teaching that count.

LESSON FROM A MOBILE FOSSIL

I LEARNED SEVERAL THINGS in college. One lesson occurred when I was a senior in a class on medieval art history. The course was taught by an extremely scholarly and extremely old professor. She knew everything about Gothic cathedrals, and we thought it was because she was there when they were built. I would sit in the back of the room, only because we were not allowed to sit in the hall. One day she showed a Byzantine picture in class and the dreaded question came from this mobile fossil. She asked, "Mr. Starbird, what do you see in this picture?"

The picture just seemed weird—the hands were too long, the head was too small, and there was a bright gold halo shining on top. I was a math major. Obviously, nothing was coming to mind. But I had been in art history classes, so I knew that art has "meaning." I tried to imitate the art analysis that I had heard, and replied, "I think the halo represents the circle of life—emerging from the darkness of the primeval void, arcing into the glory of shining heaven, and descending again into the abyss of eternity." I assure you, my answer was ripe. She said, "Cut out the bull and tell us what you see."

And that's the moral of the story. If you teach students

to be honest about what they know and what they don't know, they will transform their lives. Help students learn the habit of dealing with what they actually, personally understand instead of guessing what they think someone else wants to hear. Such intellectual honesty will completely change their lives.

> If you teach students to be honest about what they know and what they don't know, they will transform their lives.

MICHAEL STARBIRD

> *It is a teacher's responsibility to engage all students, meet them where they are, and help all of them succeed.*

THE MIRROR EFFECT

THE ATTITUDE AND ENTHUSIASM of your class is a direct reflection of how your students perceive you. If you find yourself leading a class in which your students are not properly engaged or excited about the material, try looking for answers in the mirror. The best way to improve what is happening in your class is to see yourself as your students do, then make the adjustments necessary to provide them with the image you want them to see. When I am excited about what I am teaching, my students are excited to learn it. When I am having fun in class, so are they.

> The attitude and enthusiasm of your class is a direct reflection of how your students perceive you. If you find yourself leading a class in which your students are not properly engaged or excited about the material, try looking for answers in the mirror.

Conversely, when I am not fully engaged during class, the students are not either. On many occasions over the years I have had to reboot my own attitude and enthusiasm midsemester, which has always been followed by an *immediate* improvement in the attitude and enthusiasm of the class.

I was fortunate to have this mirror effect made apparent to me even before I stepped foot in a classroom as a faculty member. When I first arrived at the University of Texas at Austin, I asked two senior colleagues for advice on teaching large organic chemistry lecture classes. One told me that I would be disappointed with student attitudes and that I should not expect students to be interested in organic chemistry. He went on to say that the students would be impossible to work with because they are focused on the wrong things. More than just a little shaken, I went to see the other colleague, who was known for teaching excellence and innovation. He told me that we were lucky to be faculty members at a major university with such enthusiastic and eager students. He was convinced our students love organic chemistry and predicted that interactions with them would be the highlights of most of my days on the faculty.

Immediately after the second conversation, I retreated to my office, shut the door, and began to process the two very different depictions of students. Knowing that both colleagues were talking about the same student population, I tried to draw a straight line between these data points. That's when it dawned on me: *in many ways, my two colleagues had just unknowingly described themselves.* Both of them *had* correctly described the students they experienced, but each one's description was a direct reflection of his own attitudes and engagement, whether positive or negative.

BRENT IVERSON

Teach like you mean it!

CURIOSITY AND
THE JOY OF LEARNING

"Curiosity is the very basis of education and if you tell me that curiosity killed the cat, I say only the cat died nobly." —ARNOLD EDINBOROUGH

YOU ARE GREAT at a variety of things and not so great at others. Have you ever asked yourself why? In most cases, you become really good or even great at what interests you. You play at tennis, math, painting, science, fishing, history, and so on, and become better because of it. You are willing to jump in and learn about something by interacting with it from the top, bottom, and left- and right-hand sides, not being too concerned about a linear sequence of thought or procedure that leads to a singular answer. It's not all work because you are interested. Wouldn't you want this to be the case in your classroom? Sometimes I think my most successful lectures are not content driven, but are instead opportunities to tap into students' "curiosity genes" and capture their interest. Everyone's curious—it's part of the human condition. Curiosity can be suppressed in formal education but is never lost. Ideally it should be nurtured both in and out of the classroom. If I can pique your curiosity, then I have you on the road to understanding the details needed for success in my class because you will play with the material. Your curiosity will be fed by engagement and rewarded by discovery.

Understandably, new instructors focus heavily on simply creating and delivering content in their courses, often losing focus on what may be their greatest role in the classroom: to inspire their students to become self-learners and critical thinkers by sharing the bigger picture and the relevance of what is being learned and by tapping into their students' innate curiosity. For example, I try to impart how the field of chemistry isn't a collection of facts and equations, despite the way it is often represented in the classroom, but is instead a story, replete with human drama, successes and failures, and conceptual connections that describe all that is going on in and around you. It is my privilege to share that story, with the testable details, facts, and equations naturally filling in around the bigger-picture skeleton. In a standardized-testing world, has the focus on testable details become the classroom model, and, if so, at what cost to the process of learning? It is my contention that students and people in general are more receptive to understanding details if they are first interested in the material; this is the joy of learning.

"It is nothing short of a miracle that modern methods of instruction have not yet entirely strangled the holy curiosity of inquiry."

—ALBERT EINSTEIN

Because of my curiosity, I began learning to play guitar at the age of forty-nine and now keep two guitars on stands in my living room for easy access, picking them up often to tinker and play. I practice frequently, which leads to moments of discovery (successful notes, chords, rhythms, and so on), further fueling my interest in learning. Contrast this experience with how most students are first introduced to playing an instrument. They are assigned one in school, perhaps a recorder or, in some cases, the instrument with the mouthpiece easiest for them to make a sound on (!), and then taught individual notes and told to practice x number of minutes each day. It is a wonder that any students continue playing music beyond the minimal school requirement! Wouldn't a better approach to teaching an instrument be to first capture student interest in the sound of music? I learned to cook because I enjoy food. I was a receptive student in the kitchen and became a self-learner because of my interest. If you want to teach someone to cook, give him or her memorable meals first. There is a pattern here. Whether an instructor wants to teach chemistry, guitar, or how to cook, he or she should first focus on capturing interest. Teachers should always serve memorable meals."

> Curiosity is fed by engagement and rewarded by discovery, which ultimately leads to learning.

Inspiring lecturers and lectures matter because they fuel the natural curiosity present in all of us. Curiosity is fed by engagement and rewarded by discovery, which ultimately leads to learning.

> *"The important thing is not to stop questioning. Curiosity has its own reason for existing. One cannot help but be in awe when he contemplates the mysteries of eternity, of life, of the marvelous structure of reality."*
>
> —ALBERT EINSTEIN

JOHN SIBERT

What makes you your students'
favorite professor?

CHANGE BEFORE YOU HAVE TO

I WISH I COULD take credit for the title of this essay, which is a quote attributed to Jack Welch, former CEO of General Electric. Although he is referring to change in business organizations, the same idea applies to teaching and learning. We are frequently confronted by myriad new teaching ideas, methods, and techniques, and it is very easy to just say the heck with it. But change is always good as long as it brings about positive and desired results.

Change has come to the media in the form of technology using names such as Facebook, Twitter, Instagram, and Snapchat. The initial reaction of most faculty members was that all these new modes of communication were just distractions. "Let's keep them out of the classroom," many of us said. While social media have changed the lives of our students for better or worse, we have been sticking up for "traditional" education and insisting that there is no place for this new "stuff" in the hallowed grounds of our universities. No way, no how, no matter what! We are just too sophisticated for something like that. Learning cannot happen on Facebook. How can you mix Mark Zuckerberg's desire for millions of dollars and world domination with learning? And just when we thought we had won the battle, here comes the bright, young, recently graduated assistant professor who knows everything, even keeping her students informed on Facebook. She ruined it for the rest of us. Where did we go so wrong?

So, who is, in fact, right? The answer is not as straightforward as it might seem. Yes, new, shiny stuff always looks better, stronger, more efficient, and more effective. But how do we really know whether that's the case? Well, rather than simply jumping on or off the bandwagon of the next version of Canvas or Blackboard or even Facebook, why not study these media and learn about them? Will these tools really change our lives and those of our students? I am all for change, and I love shiny new things as much as the next guy or gal. But how this "stuff" improves learning is not clear. It is our duty not to use something just for the sake of using it, but to use it in a way that makes sense. If you decide to adopt something new, study it in a way that allows the laggards in the group to be informed and to perhaps use it as well. As teachers, our responsibility does not stop with *our* students. If we find out about something that will help *all* students learn better, then we should certainly pass it on, share it, write about it, tweet it, and post it. Is Jack Welch right? I don't know. It depends on how good this change is. Keep sharing.

> It is our duty not to use something just for the sake of using it, but to use it in a way that makes sense.

JOHN HADJIMARCOU

Teachers don't give grades,
students earn *them.*

THE IMPORTANCE OF
ADMITTING YOU DON'T KNOW

DURING MY TEACHING CAREER, there have been many instances in which a student has asked me a question that I couldn't answer. Often, my inability to respond comes from the fact that I simply do not know the answer. In some cases, I don't know because I learned the answer long ago and have forgotten. In other cases, I don't know because I have never learned or even thought about it. I love questions I cannot answer because they indicate that the student is engaged in thoughtful consideration of the topic and because I know that I will also learn something from the exchange.

In my experience, one of the worst things you can do in a situation like this is to trivialize the student's question as unimportant or unrelated. Why discourage the student from thinking beyond the topic presented? We should encourage any and all questions even vaguely related to the subject under consideration. Such unrestrained imagination and curiosity is an important part of learning. If we trivialize the student's curiosity, we run the risk of derailing her learning experience. Every interaction with a student should be motivating in nature.

Another improper response would be to bluff your way

through an answer that you know is incorrect. Although the immediate result might appear to be the maintenance of your position as an "expert," a simple Google search will tear down that house of cards. This would likely cause the student to doubt other things you say. Trust is critical in the student-teacher relationship. The student must trust that you are giving him accurate information.

When asked a question that I don't know the answer to, my response is always "I don't know." I then praise the student for coming up with such a good question, and ask if I can think about it and get back to her. Afterwards, I make sure that I actually do so. I sometimes ask the student to also seek the answer and let me know if she finds it before I do. These are exceptional teaching opportunities that shouldn't be missed.

> When asked a question that I don't know the answer to, my response is always "I don't know."

NEIL GRAY

Do you use the Socratic method? Really?

TEACHING AND LEARNING PASSION

WHERE DOES PASSION come from? Is it intrinsic to one's personality?

An interesting phenomenon in student evaluations is their responses to the teacher's personality rather than to their own progress in the course. As the chair of my department for several years, I have noticed this trend not only in my own evaluations but also in those of my colleagues. A recurrent comment in my student evaluations, for instance, is that I am passionate about my subject and my passion is contagious. Where does passion come from? Is it intrinsic to one's personality? Are some people gifted with it while others lack it and may not ever acquire it, no matter how hard they try? Who were some of my passionate teachers? I recall only two. As an undergraduate, I did not know anything about Milton except what I had heard from my classmates—that he is just boring. And then I had a teacher who was so passionate about Milton that I actually looked forward to each class session. In yet another dreaded poetry requirement course, we all regularly conspired to rebel over the workload. But as soon as our teacher entered the classroom, she swept us away with her passion and charm. Consequently, after each class we would duly cancel our revolution.

What do these people have in common? What fuels my own passion semester after semester? Well, at least in my case, I can detect some of the components of passion. Besides love for my subject, new perspectives and the prospect of sharing them with my students make me excited about teaching any topic. At times a new perspective is so interesting that it will render meaningless an approach I had used before.

The interconnection between research and teaching is one of the components of passion. When I am working on a project for publication, I am obsessed with it. And of course I test out my new ideas with my students. I am constantly surprised to see that their lack of knowledge may enable them to have original perspectives. There are actually times when I ask them to let me take a minute to write down one of their comments. Needless to say, they get excited every time I treat them as contributors to, rather than passive recipients of, knowledge. In turn, their excitement fuels my passion.

Passion also stems from the realization that we have enabled students to grasp new information. We all know learning is a complicated and often problematic process, because our familiarity with our material sometimes makes us unaware of the students' inability to understand what we have already mastered. We may overcome some of these problems by actively engaging students in the learning process rather than by readily providing knowl-

> Passion also stems from the realization that we have enabled students to grasp new information.

edge through our lectures. For this reason, I break down my lectures into questions, which students, by collaborating with their peers in groups, answer and present to the rest of the class. I also make the groups responsible for answering questions from their classmates. This way, questions that might have otherwise remained unasked during a lecture arise during discussions with their peers. Following their responses, I discuss only the points that students have overlooked. Such a method may work in either face-to-face or online classes. In online classes, I turn questions based on the material in my lectures into wikis; the end result is equally gratifying.

Passion does have several components. Here I have been able to discuss only two, but if you think about it, I am sure you will discover many more!

SOPHIA ANDRES

Just because you teach a thing does not mean you master a thing. Being a student is for life.

LET THEM IN ON THE SECRET

ONE OF OUR PRIMARY RESPONSIBILITIES as teachers is to let our students in on the secret. That secret is whatever knowledge we are trying to convey to them.

Most people I know have some awkward memory from childhood when they were excluded from a clique, an inside joke, or a family secret that was whispered from one adult to another right in front of them. That is one of the worst feelings in the world.

They usually also have a companion memory from some point in their lives when they were mature enough to be let in on the secret: they were part of the inside joke, they joined the circle of friends, or they were trusted with some sensitive information about a family member. They felt good when they were finally old enough to be trusted with such confidential matters.

The same is true with students. Letting them in on the secret is a sign to the students that they are ready to receive precious information and that the information is important enough to be protected.

I teach classes about energy. Sometimes when I want to emphasize a point that I really want them to remember, I will ask them something like "Do you want to know the secret about refineries?" or "Do you want the truth about renewables?" The students always nod eagerly. After all, who doesn't want to know the secret truth?

By prefacing the information that way, I give them a sign that they are about to receive exclusive knowledge to which only important people are privy. This technique makes them feel special, heightens their attention, sticks in their memory, and gives them a motivation to keep coming to class. After all, where else would they go to get such valuable insider insights?

Letting them in on the secret is a sign to the students that they are ready to receive precious information and that the information is important enough to be protected.

MICHAEL E. WEBBER

We teach for free; they pay us to grade.

A VALUE OF KNOWLEDGE

WHAT MAKES A GREAT TEACHER? Much has to do with delivery. Is the professor enthusiastic, articulate, engaging, and so on? Much has to do with organization, too. Is the material presented in a logical order? But much also has to do with content. Is the material up-to-date? Is it accurate? Is it deep? The best teachers do not just know more than their students. Rather, they are content experts.

To become such an expert, you should tailor your research to mesh with your teaching. At least some studies indicate that there is no necessary connection between good research and good teaching. Many good researchers are bad teachers and vice versa. If you are a good teacher, however, you can be an even better one by doing research that relates to courses you teach. That will help ensure that your content is accurate, rich, and detailed. Doing research in your teaching areas is not essential, but it is generally helpful and is something you should always consider in deciding which research projects to pursue. Why not make that research activity do double duty? Besides, students are often thrilled when their teachers are also recognized experts in their field.

You could even write a textbook. I have had the good fortune to teach just four primary courses over the years. For each, after I taught it a couple of times, I constructed a detailed outline of the course's substantive material, organizing it in the way I thought made the most sense, although that often differed from the existing textbooks. Thereafter, I used the outline as the basis for writing a textbook for each of the four classes. When you have delved into the material sufficiently to write a textbook, you are darned close to being a content expert.

These days, writing a textbook is easier than ever before. If national publishers are not interested, you can simply publish through local copy shops. And, of course, you need not write a formal textbook. Your course materials can be a collection of written materials, links to websites and videos, and so on. The key is that you have made the materials your own. As Benjamin Franklin said, "An investment in knowledge pays the best interest." That is true for you as well as for your students.

> As Benjamin Franklin said, "An investment in knowledge pays the best interest." That is true for you as well as for your students.

ROBERT PRENTICE

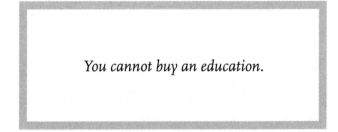

You cannot buy an education.

TEACH DOUBT

WE DON'T ACTUALLY UNDERSTAND much of anything. What we or our students now revere as core truths will often later be revealed to have some disturbing flaw—such as seeming completely wrong. In my generation's case, one belief was that we should never trust anyone over thirty. In retrospect, that perspective may not have been an example of enduring wisdom that would stand the test of time. Do your students really know why they support the collection of beliefs that they hold dear—political opinions, religious views, social habits, and so on? The answer is no, and those passionate people who have opposite opinions don't know either.

Acrimony ensues.

So here is a modest proposal for a habit you can teach your students that promotes civility and anchors us all in the reality of our own limited understanding. Every time your students state an opinion, such as "I think the death penalty is not a great idea (except, of course, for a few people I could name)," ask them to also state a percentage that expresses the level of confidence they have in their opinion. So they might say, "I think the death penalty is a bad idea. And I believe it 80%." Then if someone presents some credible evidence about how the death penalty improves the world, they could say, "Good point. I still think the death penalty is a bad idea, but now only 68%."

People who say that they are 100% certain of any opinion might as well be saying that they are closed-minded and no amount of evidence will penetrate the concrete. Such people should simply be ignored. Just getting students in the habit of realizing and acknowledging that they really are not certain and that they might adjust their opinions with evidence and experience is important. They are taking a huge step toward personal understanding and wisdom. Doubt is good.

> Doubt is good.

I believe that teaching students to embrace doubt is good advice—about 93%.

MICHAEL STARBIRD

Dare not *to teach as you were taught.*

PATIENCE IS THE MOST IMPORTANT
ELEMENT OF GOOD TEACHING

STUDENTS STRUGGLING TO GRASP an important new concept or attempting to think critically about complex issues need to know that you are not disappointed that they are having difficulty. Sometimes in my office hours or even during a lecture a student will ask a question and I will provide an answer that in my own mind is world class, ranked right up there with the most lucid explanations I have ever delivered. Instead of the complete enlightenment I might have expected, often I am confronted with an apologetic "I still don't have any idea what you are talking about" from a now increasingly hesitant student. If the issue at hand is truly important, I calmly try the explanation from a different point of view, with enthusiasm and encouragement, often stating that the concept gives many students difficulty. I will not let it go until I am *sure* the student understands.

In these situations, I remain patient and persistent above all else. I do not want the student to sense even a hint of frustration on my part that would provide him or her with an excuse to give up on him- or herself. I know that even if I am boring the rest of the students present because they had already mastered the material in question, the fact that I keep moving forward in a steadfast way sends a strong and positive signal to everyone. The entire class cannot help but understand that I want each of them to learn all of the material being presented because I think it is important that they do so.

There is an element of humility required here, and I learned this from my father when I was a teenager. My father, a brilliant Silicon Valley engineer, would often tutor neighborhood kids struggling with math. He spent a great deal of time with the daughter of my mother's hairdresser because the girl was trying to become the first member of her family to attend college. One afternoon I was in an adjacent room listening to my father calmly explain the same algebra concept to her over and over again. Never getting impatient or showing disappointment, he kept at it for a half-hour or more until the lesson was finally mastered. I was fifteen and more or less full of myself at the time. After his pupil had left, I could not help but ask my father how he could remain so patient. I said something like "How come you didn't get frustrated with her? That concept was so easy and she just didn't get it." My father responded by saying, "Why would I get frustrated? It is not easy for her." Then, after a pause, he said, "Don't forget that many things she thinks are easy are hard for you." Message received, Dad, and I am a much

> I said something like "How come you didn't get frustrated with her? That concept was so easy and she just didn't get it." My father responded by saying, "Why would I get frustrated? It is not easy for her." Then, after a pause, he said, "Don't forget that many things she thinks are easy are hard for you."

better teacher for it. I find myself relying on the wisdom of these words many times during each semester that I teach. They help me maintain a calm and patient demeanor in front of even those students who are struggling the most.

BRENT IVERSON

*Does your class help students
choose a path in life?*

I HATED GENERAL CHEMISTRY
(AND I'M A CHEMISTRY PROFESSOR!)

AS A FRESHMAN UNDERGRADUATE majoring in marine biology, I aspired to be the next Jacques Cousteau. His inspirational television specials, *The Undersea World of Jacques Cousteau*, fascinated me as a young boy. Seasonally he would take me on a one-hour trip to a world very different from mine. I didn't know how much I was learning (and I didn't care) because I was too busy enjoying the show. I also didn't realize how much teaching was taking place, teaching filled with rich content, passion, enthusiasm, communication, open-ended questions, and speculative thoughts all drawing me under the ocean. In retrospect, this was one of my earliest memories of an academically engaging experience, and it was formative.

A chemistry professor recommended that I consider changing my major to the broader chemistry degree, noting that an undergraduate degree in chemistry is more versatile than marine biology. Graduate school would then serve as an opportunity for greater specialization based on my scientific interests. Majoring in chemistry had never crossed my mind. Why not? No doubt it was because my only experience with chemistry up to that point was during freshman year when I took General Chemistry I and II, a pair of courses with minimal engagement.

Like a tall person being asked if he plays basketball, I grow weary of the reaction from others when they learn that I am a chemistry professor. The comment typically is "I hated general chemistry when I took it." After defending my discipline for a number of years, I began to respond more honestly, stating, "I hated it when I took it, too."

Why did I hate it? The learning environment in introductory chemistry (and foundation STEM classes) too often offers minimal engagement coupled with grading metrics that enforce retention of a percentage of memorized facts. That was my learning environment as a freshman. It is remarkable that anyone even cares about or wants to understand chemistry in that setting. I began to realize both the role of the professor as an ambassador for his or her discipline and the importance of engagement for student success and retention within degree plans. If the professor isn't excited about taking students on a journey through chemistry, then why should the students be? I have also come to appreciate the importance of general chemistry and other large-enrollment introductory math and science courses to the academic mission of the university. These are gateway courses that students must navigate for the university to fully open up to them. Because they are the most important classes taught in math and science departments, they must be taught well for student success and engagement.

The student-as-consumer, or economic model of education, has drawn much attention in recent years. In this model, the role of the instructor is to open the student's mind and cram as much stuff in as possible. Then, assess quickly through exams or graded work before anything falls out. It purports to provide a relatively easy and direct measure of education quality. In short, what is the immediate measurable return on the education investment? Learning is then linked to information transfer and memorized facts, but not necessarily knowledge acquisition. But there is so much more to education: the process by how you arrive at answers, the discussion and respectful debate among classmates, and the development of problem solving and critical thinking skills, all coupled to the enthusiasm, positive attitude, and engaged presence of the instructor. These critical components to a learning environment extend beyond more easily measured content-specific objectives and address the value of education in creating a more engaged student, citizen, and member of the work force.

> But one commonality among these excellent instructors is the attention that they give to academic engagement, using enthusiasm, content, and assignments to draw students into the learning environment as active participants.

Many different approaches to outstanding instruction succeed, and, indeed, many different examples of great teachers exist. But one commonality among these excellent instructors is the attention that they give to academic engagement, using enthusiasm, content, and assignments to draw students into the learning environment as active participants.

JOHN SIBERT

*Evaluating effective teaching is
critical to the evolution of learning.
How do you evaluate effective teaching?*

POSITIVE THINKING

MY FAVORITE UNDERGRADUATE professor was a brilliant historian named Phillip Paludan. What made him a truly extraordinary classroom teacher was the obvious fact that few things in life gave him more joy than teaching. Because Paludan had a gift for voices, he would sometimes transition from lecture to reenactment. He used an over-the-top British accent to explain the English view of the Revolutionary War. His Southern accent, trotted out occasionally during discussions of the Civil War, was equal parts outrageous and entertaining. Because Paludan had fun teaching, we students had fun learning.

Unlike Professor Paludan, I can't do accents. I do not try. But like Professor Paludan, there are few things in life that I find more fulfilling and more fun than teaching. So I do emulate him by making it clear to the students that I am happy to be in class and that I am having fun teaching the material, which vastly improves the odds that the students in attendance are going to have a good time and enjoy learning.

I have not immersed myself in the literature of positive psychology, but I'm pretty sure that if I did I would find scientific underpinning for what we all instinctively know—that good moods are contagious. Bad moods are as well, unfortunately. Most of us have had experiences with teachers who dearly wished to be anywhere but in the classroom. That can never end well.

So, as I toddle off to class each day, I do not focus on the grand organizational scheme that I intend to use, or the details of the most intricate concepts that I hope to impart. Instead, I simply focus on putting myself into a good mood. I used to try to think of a joke or a clever comment with which to begin class, often playing off some absurdity in the day's news. But now I am more likely to dredge up a memory of traveling to a fun place with my wife and daughters when the girls were little. Or I think about the last time I had a really good slice of chocolate cake. That's all it takes to put me in a good mood as I walk into the classroom, which is all it takes to help me set the right tone for class.

> I try to remember Herm Albright's saying: "A positive attitude may not solve all your problems, but it will annoy enough people to make it worth the effort."

No matter the course or student level, if I have a smile on my face and am in a genuinely good mood, everything will go better for me and for most of the students. Of course, there may always be a few students who are determined not to have a good time in class, no matter how positive my attitude. For them I try to remember Herm Albright's saying: "A positive attitude may not solve all your problems, but it will annoy enough people to make it worth the effort."

ROBERT PRENTICE

Students are more likely to learn from your class if they think you are fair, kind, and approachable.

IMITATE SUCCESS

I WAS RECENTLY SPEAKING to a junior colleague about one of her courses and she seemed very distraught. Neither she nor her students were excited about the course. "It's a struggle!" she pointed out. "What can I do?"

Lack of enthusiasm is as contagious as the presence of it. If you are not excited about your own course, you should not expect others (that is, your students) to be excited about it. How do you then bring the excitement back into the course? I wish the answer were easy.

> Lack of enthusiasm is as contagious as the presence of it.

Over the years, I have learned that the best way to be enthusiastic about a course is to love what you are doing. What rekindles this love is success, even the perception of it. So, how do you make your course a success in your eyes and in those of your students as quickly as possible? Although instant success is an improbable goal, you can come very close to it by imitating success. After all, the most successful companies are the best imitators. Just ask Apple and Samsung how they discovered success in the mobile phone market.

Where do you find this success? Many times it's just a stone's throw away. In my case, I have always sought the advice of colleagues who have developed a good reputation for courses that their students absolutely love. I've attended many classes of other successful colleagues to learn about the things they do in their classrooms. I have collected many tips, tactics, and strategies. Have I used all of them? No! I use only the ones that I am comfortable with that are appropriate for my class. To spice things up from one semester to the next, I introduce something new just to keep me on my toes. Some new things don't work out well and I have to make several tweaks. One more thing: I do not pretend to be someone else just to try something new. Some of these successful colleagues have used humor and even singing to bring about an environment that both they and their students enjoy. It works for them but I know it's not going to work for me.

JOHN HADJIMARCOU

Teach hard or go home.

KNOW WHAT YOU'RE TALKING ABOUT
(AND NEVER WASTE A DISASTER)

THERE IS AN UNDERLYING ASSUMPTION that if you are assigned to teach a course, you have mastery over the material. But after teaching for some time, we can look back and appreciate how much deeper and broader our understanding of the subject matter (and indeed, of the discipline) is compared to when we started as educators. The converse is that, early on in our teaching careers, we may be less aware of our limitations, and therefore less cautious in extrapolating from what we think we know.

In my first year as an assistant professor, I was assigned to teach the theory and practice of using vaccines to prevent disease. The underlying principle of vaccination is fairly straightforward. By exposing the body to the pathogen (or a part of the pathogen, or something that looks like the pathogen), the body is fooled into believing that it has been infected. The result is an immune response to this "benign invasion," but also (and more importantly) an immune surveillance that will jump into action if your body ever does see the real pathogen. With that understanding as a foundation, there's lots to talk about: many diseases, many vaccines, side effects, who decides who gets vaccinations and how often, and so forth.

A pivotal point in my teaching career came about when I covered RhoGAM that first year. RhoGAM is administered during pregnancy and at birth if the mother is Rh-negative and the fetus is Rh-positive to prevent the Rh-factor hemolytic anemia that could otherwise occur in subsequent births. After I explained this practice in class, a student asked very logically (and here it comes), "If the mother was 'vaccinated' in this pregnancy, will she need to be 'vaccinated' in subsequent pregnancies?" Without really thinking, I gave the knee-jerk response, "Of course not! She's already been 'vaccinated'!"

Classes were on Tuesdays and Thursdays, and this had happened on Thursday. That Thursday night it hit me that something about what I'd said just wasn't right. So I looked it up. RhoGAM doesn't work like a typical vaccine, and had I thought it through, I would have realized that. The one RhoGAM shot protects the mother and fetus for that one pregnancy, but everything starts over with the next pregnancy. I was wrong—dead wrong! And I had until class time the following Tuesday to anguish over my mistake and have my imagination run wild with worst-case scenarios. What if one of our pharmacy students gave birth that weekend and protested, "No, my professor said I don't need RhoGAM again!"

I was wrong—dead wrong!

Okay, that's an overreaction and an over-the-top extrapolation to a very unlikely worst-case scenario. I could have easily minimized my torment by simply correcting my mistake on Tuesday and forgetting about it, but I'm also a firm believer in never wasting a disaster (and this was one). I'm actually *glad* that it had such a profound effect on me so early in my teaching career and for the lessons it taught me. Lesson #1 is to know the facts before you lecture, although that's not enough. If I had taken the time to think through the question when it was asked, I am confident that, even in those early teaching days, I would have been able to reason through to the correct response (or at least to the reply "I'll get back with you on that"). So, Lesson #2 is to be more deliberate in thinking through student questions and sharing that critical thinking process with the students.

We all make mistakes. I've made a number of other mistakes during my years of teaching. It's what we do with those mistakes that determines whether they serve to help us grow personally and professionally. Lesson #3 is to never waste a disaster; it's an opportunity for growth.

PATRICK DAVIS

Do your students know the goals of your class?

TEACHING AND LEARNING IS BASED ON COMMUNICATION

CONNECTIONS

AS I HAVE WATCHED the evolution of remote teaching modes from radio to television to videotape to web-based MOOCs, I have remained convinced of the importance of the personal connection between teacher and student. It fosters dedication to difficult tasks, pride in success, and trust built on integrity.

At the first class of the semester I have the students fill out 5×7 cards with information to bridge the gap between us: name (including what they prefer to be called), hometown and high school, and major or academic interest. Then I ask them to include two final items I find to be particularly useful. The first is something specific about them individually, such as an interesting vacation taken, musical training they may have, unusual work or hobbies that they do, and likes or dislikes. The second is the name of a teacher, preferably in high school, who had a very positive impact on them during their precollege years, someone they would like to thank. By keeping the stack of cards handy during the semester, I have a ready resource to develop common bonds with the members of the class.

Perhaps the most important step is to learn the names of the students as soon as possible, so one should not miss an opportunity to do so: a visit during office hours, a conversation after class, or in the process of returning homework papers.

> Learn the names of the students as soon as possible.

Some years ago I would require that the students turn in their test papers directly to me, even in a large class. This allowed me to learn 15–20 new names on each test day. Fortunately the miracle of technology has made it possible for me to get a photo roster of those enrolled even before the semester has begun. It takes only a little bit of time and effort to learn many names, and this tangible, often surprising gesture translates to a lasting link with each student.

JAMES VICK

How do we bridge academic and student cultures?

WHAT'S IN A NAME?

WHAT'S IN A NAME? According to Shakespeare's Juliet, not much. Her answer, "That which we call a rose / By any other name would smell as sweet," is one of the most recognizable lines in literature. Another perspective on the importance of a name was presented in the little-known short story written by Isaac Asimov in 1956, "What's in a Name?" In this murder mystery, set in a library, a librarian was accused of the crime because of her inability to remember the name of a person who inquired at the reference desk during the time of the murder. The detective's assumption was that she could not possibly have forgotten the name, and thus must not have been present at the desk as claimed.

While I agree with Shakespeare that a person's value is independent of his or her given name, I also agree with Asimov. Remembering a person's name is an expected social courtesy with tremendous value. No matter how cursory the original introduction or how long ago, acknowledging someone by name each time you greet them is not only respectful but a critical part of advancing any relationship with that person. Remembering a person's name says, "You are important enough to me that I remembered who you are." This is especially critical in the mentor-protégé relationship between teacher and student. I have always found it disheartening to meet a student in the hallway and have her acknowledge me by name and not be able to repay the courtesy. "Hi! How are you?" is never an adequate substitute for "Hi, Amber! How are you?" The first response says, "I don't know who you are." Although subtle, it is almost always obvious that the student recognizes the omission. A short pause before the student responds is usually the clue. In such a situation, I feel that I have missed a critical opportunity to advance the relationship with that student.

> No matter how cursory the original introduction or how long ago, acknowledging someone by name each time you greet them is not only respectful but a critical part of advancing any relationship with that person.

There is nothing quite like looking across a sea of student faces only two weeks into the semester, pointing at a student in the back of the room, and saying, "Sean, what do you think?" In response, the student almost always looks around for *another* student named Sean, and, finally, with self-pointing realization, says, "Me?" This is an especially powerful tactic if you have never had a conversation with the student. His assumption was that you did not know who he was and he is amazed when you do. Although this may seem like a simple act, you have just formed a bond with that student. Furthermore, you have indirectly made several things clear:

- I recognize you as an individual in this class.
- You are memorable.

- You are not just a number.
- You can't hide in the crowd.
- Sit up straight and pay attention, because I may call on you at any time!

From a practical point of view, learning the names of one hundred students in a single class is a daunting task. Even so, I have found several successful methods. One of the best tools I have used is a series of short diagnostic quizzes, usually three. I give one quiz at the end of each of the first three lectures. There are two purposes for these quizzes. The first is to establish the students' incoming knowledge of the prerequisite course material. The second is a covert attempt at matching name to face. I get two shots for each quiz: one when the student turns it in and another when I give it back. As a chemistry teacher, I have also taken advantage of the lab to learn a student's name. Assigned seating is another method, although this is usually not well received by the students. In the end, each teacher has to develop a method that works in his or her classroom. The important thing is to do it. You won't regret the effort.

NEIL GRAY

When a student asks you a question, do you answer it clearly, concisely, and directly, or do you take the opportunity to share everything you know about the subject?

ELEVATE YOUR AUDIENCE

"These people feed me, shelter me, and love me . . . they must be God." —DOG

"These people feed me, shelter me, and love me . . . I must be God." —CAT

"These people show up just to listen to me talk and hang on every word and do what I ask . . . I must be God."
—PROFESSOR WHO SPEAKS DOWN TO STUDENTS

"These people come here just to learn so they can better themselves and improve society . . . they must be God."
—PROFESSOR WHO SPEAKS UP TO STUDENTS

ONE OF THE BIGGEST MISTAKES I see teachers and other public speakers make is to speak down to an audience. Academia in particular invites this phenomenon, because the unspoken currency on campus is intellectual superiority. Professors are known to use specialized jargon and complicated equations that are designed to show how smart they are rather than to convey the information effectively to their audience. The downside of this approach is that the students feel patronized and are likely to tune out, which inhibits their learning.

A better approach is to elevate the audience. Teachers are there to serve the students, not the other way around. Speaking up to the students grants them the respect they deserve and will invite them to participate fully. I start classes off each semester by explaining why this subject is important, and why those students are important. Although my students might not remember everything I teach, they will remember the feeling they had while learning.

> Teachers are there to serve the students, not the other way around.

"I've learned that people will forget what you said, people will forget what you did, but people will never forget how you made them feel." —MAYA ANGELOU

MICHAEL E. WEBBER

Is the respect between you and your students mutual?

STORIES MAKE YOU INTERESTING

WHEN I BEGAN TEACHING I enjoyed visiting classes taught by well-respected colleagues in a variety of fields. I was searching for the "secret" to good teaching. Most teachers I watched were substantive, well prepared, and fair. But the very best did something more—they were marvelously engaging. Every lecture was stimulating. They said or demonstrated something in each session that sparked my imagination. They talked about ideas I desperately wanted to tell others about. I left each of their classes feeling I had learned something immensely valuable.

How did they do this? My observation was that all the great teachers were splendid storytellers. They told tales that intrigued and that made important points. Every discipline had its stories: stories of discovery in the sciences, stories of leadership in the business school, and stories of great thinkers in philosophy and literature.

Many inexperienced teachers say they're not good storytellers. They may not recognize that we all have stories in us. I am not sure you can feed a young child a meal without telling stories. Have too much to drink at a party and you will probably become a storyteller.

To become a better storyteller, you need to understand

the structure of stories. It's quite simple. In a story, you have a setting. You have characters, and those characters have goals. They face obstacles but they overcome those obstacles and achieve their goals. And they learn from the experience. What are the ground rules for good stories? Stories must have a point, be told quickly, delivered vividly, and focus on things listeners understand. They must be fresh. The best stories are, to some degree, unpredictable. Students don't know what's going to happen until the end of the tale.

You must train yourself to be a story collector. When preparing lectures I always try to remember or create some story related to what I am talking about. I might turn a dry academic study into a story of exploration and discovery. (For example, some intrepid researchers [name the place and their names] wanted to study x. They were intrigued because of such and such, so they conducted a study [tell how they did it]. The results were not at all what they expected. They redid the study and changed one variable but still got unexpected results. Finally, they figured out what was really happening and today we know this useful information.) The first time I tell a tale in class it is often awkward. My timing isn't down. I tell too much or too little. But each semester I tell the story again until it becomes a compelling tale. (By the way, a real perk for faculty is that we get a new batch of students every semester. We can use our same favorite stories year after year.)

Some people are convinced they can't tell stories. If that's true in your case, then instead collect and communicate interesting factoids. Take a tour of a museum or park. What do you remember when you leave? The stories and factoids. When teaching any subject, savvy teachers find fascinating facts that most people don't know and then populate their lectures with them. When I read anything, I am always searching for interesting factoids that I can use in class. A few years ago I read a biography of Benjamin Franklin and learned that he was one of the first published gossipmongers in the United States. Indeed, he proudly defended gossiping. Who knew? Now, when I teach how common gossip is—how even famous people do it and have done it throughout history—I'll ask something like "Who was the most famous gossip columnist in the eighteenth-century United States?"

Try it out. Because you get a new audience every semester, even if you blow a few stories this semester, you can keep trying until you get them right. You'll be a more engaging teacher for that effort.

JOHN DALY

There are no bad students,
only those who require more patience.

ENCOURAGING COMMUNICATION
IN AN ONLINE CLASS

THOSE OF US who haven't taught online before often assume that unless we can see our students' faces, we can't connect with them. Although it's true that some people require a physical presence to feel genuinely connected, there are many ways to bond with students online—and it all starts with the instructor.

The best way to encourage engagement and connection in an online class is to be present yourself. Of course we show up to our face-to-face classes, and I assume we smile (at least a little) while we are there. I'm sure that we praise students for good responses and high-quality work, and I'm equally sure that we provide them with encouraging feedback when their work misses the mark.

We need to do the same in online classes. Whether in writing, videos, or audio clips, whether directed toward individual students, groups, or the entire class, the instructor is responsible for setting the standard by checking in and commenting frequently and by providing encouraging feedback. Keep the students engaged and checking back into the class by

> An instructor who is seldom present in an online class doesn't encourage students to be present either.

giving them reasons to do so. An instructor who is seldom present in an online class doesn't encourage students to be present either. And then no one is communicating with one another.

Is this to say that the instructor has to be available 24/7, as we often hear about online classes? Absolutely not! As long as you have a communication plan for the class, let students know what it is and stick to it; students will know what to expect from you and when.

You might surprise yourself and your students with the connections you are able to create. As one student recently commented at the end of an online class, "Even though I have never seen or met you in person, thanks for making my first online class so enjoyable!"

BETH BRUNK-CHAVEZ

What role do you play in student success?

TEACH SELECTIVE LYING

I READ OVER the class roll of 120 students for my sopho-more American literature course. Not one was an English major. These students were all on a forced march.

I faced two big challenges common to many core courses: (1) discovering an issue valuable to a variety of majors, and (2) creating a method of engaging students so that they might imagine themselves as colleagues of the creators of knowledge. The issue I selected was iden-tity formation. Whether in person, on paper, or on the In-ternet, students create identities. This focus worked in an American literature course because so many writers have wrestled with the question "What is an American?"

To engage the students, I lied and required them to lie selectively. I announced that there would be four guest lec-turers and represented each in a numbered column. I'll discuss two of them here. The students quickly decided that one lecturer was wealthy and one was poor.

	1	2
Lecturer's	From wealthy family	Worked as a maid;
Mother	(chauffeur, maids;	so poor she had to

	parents rented Carnegie Hall for her to perform)	dig clams to feed her children
Lecturer's Father	Owned the Packard that carried Charles Lindberg in his ticker-tape parade; Harvard graduate	So desperate for a job that he was willing to teach seven courses and drive the school's bus for $25 a week
Lecturer	Harvard graduate; spouse has given away billions of dollars; has traveled to Vienna, Lisbon, Tokyo, and many other international cities; spent more than $200,000 on his children's college education	Worked for $10 a week in Gallup, New Mexico; farmhand on sod farm; first car cost $1 (it was a stolen car); spouse was a minimum-wage cashier at a discount store

After a discussion of the columns, I admitted to the class that all the columns were the same person: me. I explained that every author we would examine did what I had done: selected facts from their backgrounds and arranged them in a way that created the desired identity. In my case, I stacked up selected facts in one column and then placed that beside a stack of contrasting facts. All the facts were true but were stripped of context. For example, my wife was a General Manager in Financial Aid for the U.S. Department of Education; all the trips were invited lectures;

we saved for fifteen years for the children's educations; and the car was a gift—by law I had to pay $1 to get the title, and when I tried to sell it I discovered it had been stolen. The students' first assignment was to do what I had done. The contrasting identities could be rich/poor, smart/dumb, musical/tone deaf—whatever was appropriate, and they could select relatives other than mother and father. The goal was to give them a taste of what the authors we were studying had done. In a small way the students would become colleagues of the authors instead of students studying a subject.

Especially in required core courses, teachers need to create ways to invite their students to imagine themselves as colleagues of the subject's creators.

My assignment could be used in any course that focuses on identity formation. But my overall point is that, especially in required core courses, teachers need to create ways to invite their students to imagine themselves as colleagues of the subject's creators. Then they might forget they are on a forced march and join the parade.

KENNETH ROEMER

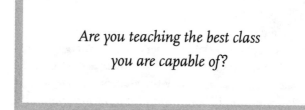

Are you teaching the best class
you are capable of?

TECHNIQUES THAT
IMPROVE LEARNING

BUY A GREEN PEN

WE ALL KNOW feedback is valuable. It helps people discover their weaknesses, understand what it takes to bol-
ster their performance, and recognize excellence. As a general rule, the more frequent the feedback, the better people
perform. Think about feedback with regard to sailing a
boat. If you get off course while sailing, but you are able to
quickly adjust because of feedback from your GPS, you'll
reach your destination. If you don't get enough feedback,
however, you'll get further and further off course.

I like to think there are two kinds of feedback. *Reinforcing* feedback tells you that you are on course. *Redirecting* feedback tells you that you're off course. You may
have played the hot and cold game as a child. Someone is
blindfolded and spun around a few times. Then the person
would set off in search of some object in the room. As she
got closer to the object, people would say, "You're getting
warmer, you are really warm." When she wandered astray,
people would say, "You're getting cold, getting colder;
you're in the Arctic." The former feedback was reinforcing;
the latter, redirecting. When conceptualized this way, all
feedback is good. The aim of both kinds is to help you find
your way more quickly. (Think about it this way: when you

drive through West Texas, any sign, even one that tells you you're heading the wrong way, is treasured.)

Both types of feedback have two components. One component is evaluative; the other is diagnostic. Evaluative feedback is the good-bad dimension. Diagnostic helps you understand the reasoning behind the evaluative feedback. The typical teaching assessment students complete at the end of a semester will ask, "Do you like the teacher?" and "Do you like the course?" These are evaluative items. They ask people to judge how good or bad the course or teacher was. The teaching assessment may also include a number of more diagnostic items, for example, "How accessible is the teacher?" or "Are lectures well organized?" or "Is technology suitable to the class?"

Which component is more helpful? For me, as a teacher, it is the diagnostic. Whether I get good or bad evaluations, I want to know why I got them. Diagnostic feedback helps me understand the evaluative reactions of students.

Now imagine a two-by-two matrix. One dimension contains the reinforcing and redirecting types of feedback; the other has the evaluative and diagnostic components. When combined, there are four cells. Now look over your recent assessments of students' work. If you're like many teachers, you'll find that when you provide students redirecting feedback, you offer both evaluative and diagnostic feedback, such as "Here is what you did wrong and let me tell you how to fix it" or "That's not exactly what the author meant. What she really meant was . . ." You use a red pen to bleed all over the presentation, paper, or exam, helping the student understand his mistakes. But when you give students reinforcing feedback, you probably offer only evaluative feedback, for example, "Great job!" or "Astute observation," or "Nice presentation!" Notice that there is no diagnostic feedback.

And that's what I want to suggest you do to improve your teaching. Go out this weekend and buy a proverbial green pen. Then, the next time you are evaluating students' performances, make sure there are as many green comments as there are red. You should be able to describe what students did and why you liked it as thoroughly as what you felt needed improvement in their work.

JOHN DALY

Remember, there are many grown-up lessons many college students have yet to learn. Be patient!

BRIDGING ACADEMIC
AND STUDENT CULTURES

BY TRANSFORMING THE THEORETICAL into the visual, we may better engage students who are now more than ever entrenched in a highly visual culture. Studies in knowledge acquisition demonstrate that we encode new information in both verbal and visual modes of memory and are better able to recall it if we can reinforce the verbal with the visual. Many foreign-language-learning programs, such as Rosetta Stone, interweave the verbal and the visual, matching words with images to facilitate the language acquisition process.

What are some of the visual media we may seek in order to make highly abstract concepts tangible? Quite a few of us rely on PowerPoint presentations to convey information concisely and clearly. But without interesting pictures to keep students engaged in the material, these presentations can be quite soporific. I often think it should be illegal to have a slide replete with words, devoid of pictures that translate the verbal into the visual. In this respect, professors in the humanities may seem to be at an advantage because they can illustrate the literary or the historical with paintings, photographs, and videos.

But the visual is a powerful and indispensable tool in

the sciences as well. I recently attended a lecture, "The Future of the Brain," by Michio Kaku, a professor of theoretical physics. As an English professor, I expected to be introduced to highly complex concepts that I might only partially understand. Yet, I was fascinated by his ability to convey the sophisticated ideas of physics to a general audience. Watching him lecture, I tried to absorb both the concepts he taught and his mode of delivery. Yes, he did rely on a PowerPoint presentation but it was not full of diagrams of the brain. Bright, colorful reproductions of well-known photographs, paintings from pop culture, and images from popular movies illustrated recent discoveries and advances in physics, making them lucid and entertaining.

Instead of criticizing our students' obsession with the Internet, we can actually capitalize on it. We may have students come up with their own visual examples that illustrate theoretical concepts we discuss in our lectures. They might seek these images in the movies or the YouTube videos they watch. YouTube videos may at times also serve as our point of departure for lectures on any subject, asking students to view them critically, for instance, by concentrating on the gaps or inconsistencies in the material conveyed. By having students engage in and critically examine works of the past or the present, we may enable them to extricate themselves from the tyrannical power of written works or social media.

> Instead of criticizing our students' obsession with the Internet, we can actually capitalize on it.

We may further involve students in creative projects that turn abstract academic concepts into personal experiences. I often ask my students to create their own YouTube video illustrating a highly complex theory with paintings, photographs, and even music. I am frequently astonished with the results and let students know how impressed I am.

Through such projects, we can also learn from our students and better communicate with them by entering their world. Simultaneously, by activating their creative resources, we may empower them to be active contributors to rather than passive recipients of knowledge.

SOPHIA ANDRES

Teaching and conducting research involve two different skill sets.

FEEDBACK SEPARATES GOOD
TEACHERS FROM MASTER TEACHERS

TEACHING IS ONE OF THE great joys in life. The feeling of leading a class through a spirited roundtable discussion that goes deeper than expected is very satisfying. Watching students have aha moments in class is rewarding. Delivering a passionate, well-orchestrated lecture with students hanging on every word can be a thrilling form of performance art that refreshes a soul. Let's face it—teaching is fun.

Grading? That's another story. Most faculty I know dread the tedium of grading hundreds of exams or papers. When finals are over, students feel relief. Teachers feel overwhelmed by the stack of projects and tests awaiting their green pens. The prospect of reading fifty papers on the exact same topic wears on the soul and makes pounding headaches seem fun by comparison. But this is the stage that separates master teachers from good teachers.

Good teachers laboriously design their curricular approach to capture a student's imagination, keep them engaged, and open their minds to new ideas. Good teachers practice their lectures, polish their presentations, and tune in to the students during class so that they can adjust their teaching in real time. These are all excellent things to do.

But master teachers do all that and more. Master teachers also invest just as much effort to polish, fine-tune, and think through their approach to assessing students and delivering feedback.

> Master teachers offer words of explanation rather than just checkmarks and cross-outs.

A good teacher will mark mistakes in papers or exams as a way to assign the student a grade. A master teacher will do that too, but will also give more explicit feedback about *why* it is wrong or what could have been done better. Master teachers offer words of explanation rather than just checkmarks and cross-outs. That feedback is a tool for assessment *and* teaching. It also takes a lot of time and thinking, which is why many teachers take shortcuts at this step.

From a good teacher, students will enjoy class and learn many things. From a master teacher, students will get all that, but they will also learn how to think.

MICHAEL WEBBER

What do you take away from your student evaluations?

MODELING CRITICAL
THINKING FOR STUDENTS

I HAVE RECEIVED GREAT GUIDANCE about teaching from colleagues over the years, but few pieces of advice have had as deep and long-lasting an impact as the simple idea of taking the time in class to model critical thinking for students.

What's the typical Q&A scenario? The student asks a question; the faculty member answers. What typically goes through the student's mind is that the professor is effortlessly and spontaneously spewing forth this wisdom because "they know all that stuff." After all, we're the ones teaching it, right?

In some cases (as with factual answers to fact-oriented questions) we probably are answering quickly and easily because we can. But in many cases, the faculty member is critically thinking through the question and synthesizing a response. This process is entirely invisible to the students, who naturally come to the conclusion that the faculty member simply already knew the answer to the question. In contrast, consider this approach: "That's a great question; let me think it through. I know x is true because . . . I also know y is true because . . . I'm not absolutely sure about z but I believe it would also be true given the following . . . My conclusion is that . . ."

Rather than concluding that the professor simply knew the answer or being mystified by how the professor came to his conclusion, most students come to the revelation "Wow, I could have done that!" From the standpoint of the learner, that feeling is empowering!

> "Wow, *I* could have done that!"

I believe I have received more positive feedback from students on this simple approach than on any other that I use in class, be it lecture, lab, discussion, or one-on-one instruction. I would love to give credit to the colleague who gave me this simple yet powerful idea, but it was so long ago that I don't remember. I also had no idea that it would have such a positive impact on my teaching and on student learning over the years.

PATRICK DAVIS

Always consider your learner's characteristics, interests, experience, learning style, and goals. What does this imply about repeating the same course every time you teach it?

TEACHING INVENTION
THROUGH IMITATION?

SINGERS DO IT. So do scientists, artists, athletes, business leaders, carpenters, and preachers. In practically all professions, people learn by imitating. If the models are exceptionally good, then imitation is often an excellent way to learn. Certainly some of the best writers started out imitating.

"Started out"—there's the rub. In American culture, imitation isn't enough. To be successful, one has to go beyond modeling to innovation. In composition classes and especially in creative writing classes, teachers place emphasis on discovering one's own style, voice, and subject. America's most famous writers may have started out modeling other writers, but they became famous because they went beyond their models. Hemingway gave Twain a twentieth-century voice, and Toni Morrison expanded Faulkner's South.

I knew that any creative writing course I proposed would have to be "innovative" to compensate for my utter lack of credentials. Unfortunately, I was old-fashioned and believed strongly in modeling. What I needed was some form of "inventive modeling" for my autobiographical writing class. I needed a model that was well written—

with vivid detail, created scenes, and an engaging narrative—and presented an intriguing way to represent the self. But I also wanted one that made simple copying of topic, style, and viewpoint difficult, and one that was initially a bit confusing, so that students had to ponder how the model worked and how they might apply its methods to their life stories.

The Way to Rainy Mountain, by the Pulitzer Prize–winning author N. Scott Momaday, became my model. The twenty-four stories in the book are each told in three interrelated but separate paragraph-length voices—a Kiowa and family storytelling voice, a historical/factual voice, and a personal memory voice. Together they demonstrate that creating a written self necessitates multiple angles of vision. There are Native American students at the University of Texas at Arlington, but none have been Kiowa from rural Oklahoma. Students can't just copy Momaday's place and culture. And the structure of the book is confusing enough that they must puzzle over how they can adapt Momaday's writing processes and vary his form to fit their lives.

Inventive modeling can be effective as long as the model represents good writing and demonstrates interesting ways to portray the self, but also minimizes the possibility of mechanical copying and maximizes the possibility that students will be confused and intrigued enough by the text to imagine how they can be inventive.

Since the 1970s when I began teaching and writing about inventive modeling and *The Way to Rainy Mountain*, my suggestions have been taken up in many colleges (even by all the entering students at one university), by students in Japan and other countries, and by inmates in a New Mexico prison. The method can be adapted to whole-semester courses or to short assignments. For instance, students can use interrelated family stories, factual information, and personal memories to create just one three-voices section.

I'm a devotee of Momaday's book. But inventive modeling doesn't depend on one book. Inventive modeling can be effective as long as the model represents good writing and demonstrates interesting ways to portray the self, but also minimizes the possibility of mechanical copying and maximizes the possibility that students will be confused and intrigued enough by the text to imagine how they can be inventive.

KENNETH ROEMER

Help students become sensible people,
and they will make themselves sensible
doctors, lawyers, and citizens.

EMBRACE THE FUBU OF TEACHING

IF THE BEST TEACHING is student-centered, then the best teachers are often our students. Indeed, some of the best learning can be achieved by adopting the principle of "FUBU" ("for us, by us"). In a FUBU universe, students become the primary agents of their own learning by providing feedback and creating artifacts that emerge out of their own experience ("by us") for their own benefit ("for us").

> In a FUBU universe, students become the primary agents of their own learning.

Consider the FUBU-ness of the "muddiest-point" card activity. This technique requires a stack of index cards, a minute of class time, and five to twenty minutes of your attention. At the end of class, distribute the index cards and invite students to write what they feel is the muddiest point of that day. You could ask them, "Which of today's concepts, theories, definitions, explanations, or examples do you still not quite get?" Encourage them to keep things simple: don't overthink, don't write more than a sentence, and don't include their name. As the students depart, they drop their anonymous cards into a box by the door (part of the ritual that I think is small but meaningful). Through this exercise, you ensure that they exit thinking about the day's learning and you end the session with valuable formative data about how to start the next class.

When you do meet next, preface any review with an explicit acknowledgment of their contribution to the process: "Thank you for sharing your thoughts about the muddiest point in our last class meeting. Before we forge ahead with *today's* class, I want to address the most commonly raised muddiest point by asking you all this: (insert relevant question here)." Then let them talk it through for a few minutes, guiding the discussion only as necessary and, if possible, creating a segue into the current day's content.

A powerful variant of the muddiest-point exercise can be implemented about a week before an exam. In this FUBU activity, you hand out larger notecards and invite students to spend the last ten minutes of class flipping through their notes from past weeks, identifying material that isn't so clear. Rather than limiting them to a single muddy point, raise the limit to five. At the end of ten minutes, dismiss the class, inviting them to deposit their cards into the box. Upon returning to your workspace, fire up your electronic device and transcribe what you've received, taking care to organize the material by grouping like comments and moving the most commonly cited items to the top of the list. You can then disseminate this compilation of muddy points as a "FUBU study guide." This study guide should *not* contain any attempt by you to teach. Refrain from any editorializing: no tips, comments, hints, or references. Simply collate, organize, and share. How they choose to use the information in the FUBU study guide is up to them. Sure, you might encourage your students to gather outside of class in small groups to discuss the items as means of preparing for the exam—and maybe even learning the material—but from there, they own the process.

DAVID SILVA

When and why did you come to love your subject area?

TO GROUP OR NOT TO GROUP

YES, THAT IS THE QUESTION! Some professors rave about the amazing results that occur when students in small groups engage in interesting and productive discussions, but other professors complain that such grouping is a waste of precious class time that could otherwise be spent in more useful endeavors. Both are true. When properly designed and structured, the small-group process in the university classroom can allow participants to operate at the highest levels of Bloom's Taxonomy, but ill-formed and poorly designed groups really can be a waste of time and leave everyone unhappy.

Imagine a freshman student in a large class being asked to answer aloud a thought-provoking question, or a shy international student being required to examine the assumption beneath a principle being espoused, again in front of everyone. The student has two issues to grapple with—his attempt to think about and respond appropriately to the question, and his potential anxiety about speaking in front of the class, particularly if it is large. I recently talked to an international undergraduate who said his heart pounded so hard when he had to speak aloud to the rest of the class that he was unable to speak at all. That might be an extreme case, but the point is that it is easier for most students to talk openly and spontaneously with three to six other students than in front of an entire class.

Reasons small groups fail include a lack of experience by the students in how to interact without being either dominating or silent; not having everyone clearly understand the purpose or goal to be accomplished and the time limit for doing so; failure of the professor to walk among the small groups as they are interacting to be sure everyone is on task; failure to provide the opportunity for the groups to report to the full class in some appropriate way; and, finally, failure to make sure that the chairs and desks of the members are all facing one another. Suggestions to make small groups even more effective are to appoint a facilitator for each group along with a brief job description of what a facilitator does, to provide paper copies of the case or the problem to each group, and to determine in advance the composition of each group. Although the easiest way to create groups is just to count off by the total number of groups to be formed, it is sometimes useful to create them in other ways—by experience, by majors, by ability, and so on.

Another problem that can be encountered is how to measure or evaluate the work that students do in the small groups. If the groups are being used only to break up interactive lectures, this activity in itself is valuable. If, however, the groups are assigned problems, projects, or cases, as in problem-based learning, grading can be more challenging. A good solution is to give both a group grade on the overall product and an individual participation grade on the total contribution each student made to the group's outcome. Published forms are available that allow group members to make judgments on the contributions of individuals.

Finally, it is useful for the professor to be prepared to justify to the class that, in most jobs, there will be the requirement to work collaboratively with others to make plans and solve problems. Interacting effectively in small groups at the university level is a great way to develop skills needed for many future endeavors.

MARY LYNN CROW

> It is useful for the professor to be prepared to justify to the class that, in most jobs, there will be the requirement to work collaboratively with others to make plans and solve problems.

I've come to believe that teachers often make terrible students, but students often prove to be highly effective teachers.

DRAWING ATTENTION
IN THE MODERN CLASSROOM

I THINK MOST TEACHERS would agree that technological breakthroughs have changed the modern classroom for the better. Such innovations have added many tools to the teacher's toolbox that have changed the way we teach, the way students learn, and how we communicate with our students. Even though many of these benefits are obvious to me now, that was not always the case. It took some time for me to discover technologies that worked for the content I teach. Chemistry involves solving equations, drawing complicated chemical structures, and properly writing reaction mechanisms. These kinds of drawing and writing skills are also important in other disciplines, such as mathematics, engineering, physics, and art. In such disciplines, it is critical that students learn to be proficient at these tasks by doing them. I always relate practical skills such as drawing and writing to carpentry—you have to hammer more than a few nails to learn the trade.

> I always relate practical skills such as drawing and writing to carpentry—you have to hammer more than a few nails to learn the trade.

A perfect time to combine the teaching and practice of these basic skills is during class. Writing and drawing complicated structures and processes while students do the same gives them the opportunity to learn the proper technique through imitation. Early in my career, I taught these skills using chalk talks. As new technology evolved, projectors and computers became a normal part of every classroom, often at the expense of blackboard space. As a result, PowerPoint presentations were more commonplace. In my case, however, digital slide presentations just didn't have the same teaching power as lessons done by hand. I was forced to look for other ways to present the material and, in hindsight, couldn't be happier that I did. Thanks to advances in tablet computing and drawing software, I finally found a digital classroom that works for me. I can't imagine going back to the old blackboard.

I now teach primarily on a tablet computer with One-Note installed. Everything I draw on the tablet is projected on a large screen at the front of the room. With all the variations in pen color and style, such presentations can be made attractive and colorful. This digital blackboard provides many advantages over the traditional one.

- The tactile feedback of the screen is very much like a thick pad of paper. The result is a more natural drawing surface and better drawings than on a traditional board.
- A wide variety of colors and line thicknesses results in cleaner drawings that are easier to interpret for students. It also allows the use of color to focus attention on a specific part of the drawing.
- Everything written on the screen can be saved as a PDF file and placed online for students to access later. I also keep a record of every lecture that I do. After class, I will annotate the lecture to remind myself of things I

want to change for next semester. This has helped me a great deal in assessing and improving my teaching.

• Integrating other technologies is easy. I often use computational software, chemical modeling software to demonstrate molecules in 3-D, and spreadsheets to teach the handling of large data sets. Switching between the various packages is seamless.

• The tablet can also be used for group activities in which students come to the front of the classroom to solve team problems.

If you are like me and must teach material that involves drawing complicated images during class and you feel trapped on the blackboard, then give the tablet computer a try. If you do, I strongly advise that you use a tablet with a screen that works with an active stylus rather than with a passive one. Whereas an active screen responds only to the stylus, a passive screen responds only to touch. Some modern devices respond to both methods of input but give priority to the pen. These devices are ideal for the classroom. All iPads and similar devices have passive screens and are not the best for drawing.

NEIL GRAY

Babies and animals learn through play.
Does play have a role in the formal classroom?

BUILD IT AND THEY WILL COME

THE TASK OF DESIGNING AND BUILDING a house is daunting, especially if it is your first time to do so. Teaching a class is like building a house. The best way to start is to draft a plan for your course. As you design your course, think it through carefully, as an architect does when she drafts a house plan. Envision the end result and then work your way backward by considering the details for each section of your course. Just as an architect needs to consider issues such as flow and functionality, you also need to consider how everything fits together.

There are too many considerations to be left to chance. What do you want your house to look like? How many bedrooms and bathrooms, and how do they fit together to provide a livable and functional space for your family? Do their opinions matter? Of course they do, if you want them to live with you. Be sure, then, to get their input early on in the process. What if some things don't work out after you have built this house? Don't be afraid to remodel. Eventually you will reach the stage at which you have a very comfortable house and you will be proud of the effort that you have put into it.

Similarly, there are many considerations when designing and building a course. But knowing what the end result needs to look like (that is, what your students need to know and be able to do by the end of the course) is a very good start. Then, you simply put the pieces together to get there. Most architects start with a stock plan and then tweak it to meet their clients' desires. You don't have to reinvent the wheel—don't be afraid to imitate the good work of your colleagues. All you need to do is to ask for their help and you will flatter them. You must also change the stock syllabus to meet your needs and those of your students. Most importantly, make the design such that it is comfortable to teach the course. After all, if you don't like your own course, what is the point? Just like an architect, be sure to ask your students for feedback. You do not have to make all the changes the students would like to see, but most of the time their comments are useful.

> Any course design is a good design as long as it is simple, functional, and gets the job done with the least amount of effort.

Other teachers frequently ask me, "What is a good course design?" My answer to that question is straightforward. Any course design is a good design as long as it is simple, functional, and gets the job done with the least amount of effort. Oh, and by the way, anyone should be able to pick up your syllabus and understand how and why all the elements of the course fit together. Can you imagine a house without a bathroom or a door leading into and out of each room?

JOHN HADJIMARCOU

Can you teach if you are not an expert?
Can you coach if you have never played?

CONTAINING THE
CLASSROOM HIJACKER

EVERY ONCE IN A WHILE, I get a student who believes that I serve as his private tutor performing before a live audience. Such a student commonly assumes full responsibility for answering whatever question I pose to the class. Oblivious to those around him, this "hijacker" thrives on the opportunity to (over-)share to a captive audience. Allowed to persist, a successful hijacker can undermine the relationships crucial to effective learning—with each public pronouncement, he simultaneously feeds his ego, alienates his classmates, and frustrates his teacher. What to do?

I use the "Listen, Write, and Read" method, as explained in the following list.

1. *Announce.* "Everybody take out paper and a pen," you can tell your students. (This might be a shock to those taking notes on a laptop, but the act of putting pen to paper is a valuable experience for twenty-first-century students, especially if you administer in-class exams in this nineteenth-century method.)

2. *Explain.* Say, "I'm going to ask you all a question. Take a minute to think about it and write down your thoughts."

3. *Ask.* Pose the question.

4. *Monitor.* For the next minute, traverse the room, ensuring that people are actually writing stuff down. If you find that students aren't writing, encourage them. (The first few times you do this exercise, you'll have to convince your students that you really do expect them to think *and* write.)

5. *Invite.* Once the listening and writing are done, identify a student and ask, "Please read what you've written." It's important that you are explicit in this request ("read what you've written") so that the student doesn't speak extemporaneously, which is precisely what you're avoiding right then and there.

6. *Repeat.* Once the first student has read what he or she has written, ask a second to do the same, then a third. Keep the request focused on "reading what you've written."

7. *Expand.* At some point, you might open the discussion by asking, "Who's written something different from what you've all heard?" When a student does raise a hand, honor the procedure by saying, "Great! So what did *you* write?"

Using Listen, Write, and Read, you can manage a hijacker by enforcing rules that apply to everybody. If, for example, the hijacker interrupts, simply tell him, "Hold on a second; it's so-and-so's turn." When it comes time to acknowledge the hijacker, invite him to read what he's written. When he begins to speak "off book," enforce the central rule to "read what you've written."

This method has proven extremely useful. First and foremost, it puts you back in control. Second, it signals to the class that you value universal participation. Third, it allows you to acknowledge the hijacker, but with boundaries. Fourth, it provides opportunities for shy or insecure students to contribute to the discussion with the safety net of a "script." (This point is especially relevant for limited-

English students whose linguistic and cultural incompetencies may inhibit participation.) Finally, this practice reinforces a key principle of learning: that writing helps thinking and thinking helps writing.

The third or fourth time you implement this practice in your classroom, you'll notice new behaviors emerging. I've been particularly struck by how my students perk up when I say, "Take out something to write with." They know what to expect: to listen, to write, to read—and to be part of the discussion.

DAVID SILVA

Did you smile at your students in class today?

LISTENING FOR SILENCES

WHAT HAPPENS WHEN you ask a question of a class full of students, and . . . no . . . one . . . answers? You look around the room to find that all eyes are averted from your gaze. "If I make eye contact with her," they think, "she will surely call on me to answer that question." Some of us may be perfectly fine waiting for a response, asking the question in another way. But many of us, I suspect, would prefer to fill up that silence with answers.

Putting aside our own discomfort with silence, we wonder what could be happening here. It's possible that students need a few moments to process a response to your brilliant, thought-provoking question. It's possible that they simply aren't prepared to answer. It is also possible that your question was, well, not a good question. And then what happens if we jump in and answer it for them? What message does that send?

Over the years, I've found a number of ways to either structure a less silent class or be comfortable with silence. Asking students to do more than read the textbook or articles before class is one good solution. Ask them to write a response to the reading, to participate on a discussion board, or to work in small groups before a larger class discussion. All of these activities help students think through the content before you pose those thought-provoking queries. When students have had a chance to think through some ideas and articulate them in other ways, they may then feel more comfortable sharing with the larger group.

Additionally, learn to be comfortable with silences yourself. Tell the students, "I'm going to let you think about that." Then count to ten slowly. Take a few sips of coffee and move around the room a bit. Pose the question again, and then see what they come up with.

> Learn to be comfortable with silences yourself.

Silences can be telling. That's true in relationships, in politics, and in teaching. Learning to listen carefully to the silences—and noticing when they occur—will help us move beyond frustration and discomfort. It will assist us in figuring out the best way to help students think deeply and articulate their thoughts.

BETH BRUNK-CHAVEZ

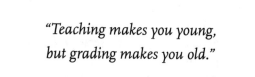

"Teaching makes you young,
but grading makes you old."

COLLEGE STUDENTS NEED
TO LEARN HOW TO LEARN

HOW YOU THINK IS
JUST AS IMPORTANT AS
WHAT YOU THINK ABOUT

METACOGNITION IS THINKING about thinking. Students don't often think about thinking. But they need to learn how. One good way to get students to consider *how they are thinking* as well as *what they are thinking about* is to give them brief daily or weekly self-assessment assignments. Ask them to take a few minutes at the end of class, or at the end of the week, to answer questions such as these:

> What helped me learn today?

- What did I learn today (or this week)?
- What questions do I still have about what we did in class today (or this week)?
- How does the new information I have learned relate to other things I know?
- What helped me learn today (or this week)?
- What got in the way of my learning?
- When I start my homework for the next class, what should I take from today's lesson?
- Are there ways to apply what I am learning in this class to other classes or situations?

Have students keep these metacognitive assessments in a notebook that they keep with them in class. From time to time, in the middle of class, ask them to take these notebooks out and scribble in them for five minutes. Use what they write to talk about how to think critically, what gets in the way of critical thinking, and how they can improve.

CATHERINE ROSS

Is teaching beyond the classroom important?

TEACH YOUR STUDENTS HOW TO MASTER THE MATERIAL PRESENTED

WE OFTEN ASSUME our students know how to study or otherwise learn the material we are presenting, but this is often not the case for freshmen or even sophomores. Transitioning from high-school to college-level work means students must approach their studies in entirely new ways. Some students figure this out on their own, but many do not. In my case, few of the students entering my organic chemistry class have ever tackled the subject before. I have therefore spent a great deal of time developing approaches and techniques to aid student learning, and these are presented to students along with the course material. Although the following is specific to organic chemistry, I hope the detailed descriptions can inspire analogous approaches in other technical disciplines.

My course website provides a detailed description of suggested approaches to studying as well as a summary of tips shared by former students who were successful in the class. I use my own end-of-semester survey to track trends in the way my students are preparing for exams and doing homework. My first lecture of the semester emphasizes and summarizes suggested best practices such as weekly outlining of lecture notes and creating ever-expanding lists of specific concepts or formulas. Similarly, I use the concept of a two-dimensional "road map" to help students identify in graphic form the important connections and relationships among the many dozens of different chemical reactions they learn during the semester.

Content delivery in class has also been modified to aid in mastery and retention of the material. For example, I emphasize understanding and learning (as opposed to memorizing) complex reaction mechanisms using a unique process in which students are taught how to choose each individual step from a set of four specific mechanistic elements, enabling the accurate *prediction* of multistep mechanisms. The approach is reinforced continually during lecture. I also show students how to identify "Key Recognition Elements" of molecules that provide guideposts for how to synthesize a given complex structure from simpler component molecules (the entire point of organic chemistry, by the way).

My goal is to create a comprehensive academic experience for students in which they "learn how to learn my content." It takes effort to equip them with the skills needed to master the large amount of technical course material I throw at them, but it is worth it. Former students have often told me that learning these approaches in my class paid dividends throughout their undergraduate years and be-

> For students, learning how to master large amounts of complex material greatly transcends the importance of the specific content of my class.

yond. For students, learning how to master large amounts of complex material greatly transcends the importance of the specific content of my class.

BRENT IVERSON

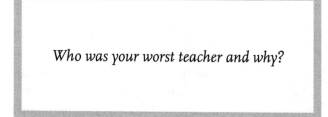

Who was your worst teacher and why?

MAKE THEM ACCOUNTABLE, BUT DO IT KINDLY

STUDENTS HAVE TO BE READY for the work of learning, and they have to be held accountable. In most cases, to be successful at a university, students need four things: they need to know the purpose or usefulness of their studies, they need to have time to do the work, they need to know how to do that work, and they need to do it. How can you help?

First, take the time to explain *why* your course is important; students don't always see the big picture. Do this more than once, and do it with excitement. Second, give them a reasonable amount of time to do their assignments; remember that they have three or four other classes, probably a job, and maybe a family. Third, be sure to model the reading, thinking, and problem-solving skills you expect them to use to complete their assignments. Don't assume they already know how to do these things. (If you have Blackboard available, you can set up a practice quiz or a set of study questions for each assignment so that students can check their progress while they are doing their work.)

Finally, hold them accountable *every day*. Build a series of brief daily quizzes into your course grading structure. Five straightforward, factual questions each day are all you need.

Once students get used to this process (and get over being resentful of the daily quizzes), they will begin to develop self-discipline, to experience the relief of being ready for class, and to know the pleasure of having something worthwhile to add to the discussion.

CATHERINE ROSS

Go beyond what your students expect of you.

UNDERSTANDING FAIRNESS

LIFE ISN'T ALWAYS FAIR. But people believe it should be. People in the working world complain that their bosses play favorites. Children "know" their sibling is the favorite child. This sense that things aren't fair often pervades classrooms too. When I began teaching, figuring out how to treat students fairly occupied a lot of my thinking. One of my goals as a teacher was to have students come up at the end of a semester and say something like "I really learned a lot and liked what you taught, even though I ended with a C. It's what I deserved."

So, being an academic, I went to the research. I found that one kind of fairness is called *procedural*. Simply put, when people believe the processes used to make judgments are fair, they can live with almost any outcome, even when that outcome doesn't benefit them. Parents know this: if your kids agree to the ground rules (for example, "No McDonalds" and "Take turns on the Xbox") before leaving on a road trip, then when what they want doesn't happen you can reference the ground rule (for example, "Didn't we agree before we left that house that . . . ?").

Here are a few ways I try to demonstrate procedural fairness in my classes.

First, I am consistent with the rules I establish for the class. I tell students at the start of the semester what they need to get a good grade and then I stick with it.

Second, I give students two chances on each test. Because my major undergraduate class enrolls about four hundred students each semester, I use multiple-choice exams. I have a midterm and a final. Let's say that the midterm, composed of sixty questions, is scheduled for October 15. On October 22, students can take what we call a retest, composed of different questions covering the same material. Students are required to take only one of the two tests. But we advise them to take both. Why? Because we record only the higher of the two grades. Students get a second try to show what they have learned. This makes the testing process fairer, since some of the variability in student performances on exams is due to the particular ways teachers create their exams. It also makes tests fairer in another way. Sometimes students tell me that they had a bad day when the test was scheduled—a boyfriend dumped them, they were sick, they had another exam, and so on. With the retest, I can say, "No problem, just take the retest."

Parenthetically, retests also offer an academic benefit. Call it the testing effect. Studying for an exam once helps students integrate and remember the content of lectures. Doing it twice helps them integrate and remember even more.

Third, I offer clear and unambiguous instructions for assignments. (Don't do what a former colleague did: offer vague instructions and then when asked for clarification by students, say, "I can't really explain what I want but I'll know it when I see it.")

Fourth, I try to make sure that students are assessed by what they know and not simply how they can game my tests. In every class, some students will complain that they've read too much into some test questions. So, on test day in my classroom, students receive, in addition to the exam and the Scantron, a blank piece of paper that they submit when they are finished. On that paper, students can identify items they felt were ambiguous. For those items, they describe both why they chose the answer they did and why another answer might be the right one. After each test we have a half-day session during which students can drop in and review their exams. If students find that they missed an item they wrote about, they can approach the teaching assistants and show them that, indeed, they knew the right answer. My goal with this method is to make sure we fairly assess what students know rather than how well they can interpret questions. More broadly, I try not to confound the substance of what I assess with my method of assessment—for example, do shy students really need to be forced to talk in front of others to demonstrate their knowledge of, say, economics?

There are certainly many ways to demonstrate fairness. What's important is to make sure students always know that you care enough to be fair in how you judge them.

JOHN DALY

Information, especially in technical fields, can become obsolete, but a teacher's inspiration often lasts a lifetime.

CREATING A SAFE ZONE
IN THE UNIVERSITY CLASSROOM

HOW DID YOU FEEL when you first entered a college classroom to face an all-knowing professor and lots of new students, all of whom might know more than you about this course? Memories may dim, but each of us can probably remember what our first university course or first class meetings in general felt like. Maybe we had lots of different feelings, but *safe* was probably not among them. It's hard to determine the single most important variable a student needs for learning to be successful, but a good candidate would be safety, because for one to become vulnerable enough to grow and learn, one must first feel safe. Let's not, however, confuse safety with a lack of excitement or intellectual stimulation. Safety does not imply boredom or passivity. There clearly must be a balance in the classroom between psychological security and creative tension.

> For one to become vulnerable enough to grow and learn, one must first feel safe.

Students who fear what the professor or the other students will think of them, or who fear the consequences of asking a dumb question or giving a wrong answer, are more motivated to defend and protect themselves than to be open to learning something new. Simply put, people don't usually learn when they're afraid, and any learning that might occur is typically not academic. If learning can be defined as the ability to grow, change, and make new adaptations and accommodations, then students who are stressed or anxious will find it difficult to learn. Abraham Maslow's well-studied hierarchy of needs indicates that if the lower-level safety needs are not met, then one is unable to proceed further up the ladder to where learning or actualizing would occur.

There are a number of things a professor can do to create this safe zone and, of course, an equal number of things it is better not to do. Keep in mind how different our Texas classrooms can be. One can find a wide variety of cultures and races, ages, personalities, first languages, socioeconomic and experiential backgrounds, abilities and disabilities, values and work ethics, and short- and long-term goals. Creating a safe zone that will incorporate all these differences while still teaching content and maintaining high academic standards is not easy. It is, however, well worth the considerable effort involved.

What usually feels safe to most students is for the professor:

- to be respectful of what she may consider to be dumb questions,
- to be available outside of scheduled class meeting times,
- to remember that sometimes students can explain something to the class even better than she can,
- to allow students to interrupt her when she has used a term they are not familiar with or that she has pronounced differently from them,

- to provide opportunities for students to interact with other students,
- to allow students to offer explanations in their own words or to give examples,
- to call students by their names,
- to adapt her rate or speed of speaking to a learning situation (as opposed to a social situation),
- to give supportive reinforcement when appropriate, and
- to be approachable.

What usually does not feel safe to students is when the professor:

- uses threats or scare tactics to motivate,
- compares students or classes to one another,
- is sarcastic,
- embarrasses them,
- doesn't return assignments promptly,
- changes the syllabus without notification,
- doesn't return emails or show up for office hours, and
- is more focused on what she's doing or saying in the classroom than on what her students are learning.

Creating a psychologically safe zone in the university classroom is worth whatever it takes to your students.

MARY LYNN CROW

Are students qualified to evaluate teaching?

TEACH EFFECTIVE THINKING

THE CORE PURPOSE of the University of Texas at Austin is "to transform lives for the benefit of society." The core purpose is not to award degrees, to give grades, or even to teach students what is now known. The core purpose is to transform lives. That transformation refers to developing the potential of our students to become more able members of the world community. Our challenge is to empower our students to solve problems, including many that may not even exist today. How can we succeed in the daunting task of preparing students to be able to address challenges beyond those we can dream of?

The answer is that we must teach students to become lovers of lifelong learning and to become effective thinkers—that is, to become people who think creatively and insightfully out of habit.

Keeping that clarity of purpose at the forefront of our minds informs daily decisions in our classrooms. We might resist the temptation to impose one more unpleasant requirement in an effort to coerce students to cover the packed syllabus. Instead, we might allow students the luxury of the joyful exploration of fundamental ideas. We might design class experiences so that students model independent and creative thinking, including making errors, raising questions, and anticipating the flow of ideas.

The class that had the most impact on me during my own formal education was one I took in my first year of graduate school. The course was taught in a manner that I considered quite odd at the time. We students were presented with a list of theorem statements and exercises. We were told that our job was to prove the theorems on our own using no resources other than our minds. For the first several weeks I sat in the back of the room watching other students present their work at the board. Even though the format of the class had been clearly described, it did not occur to me that I was really expected to prove the theorems. I had never before proved theorems on my own. I remember a moment in the class several weeks into the semester when one of the exercises was particularly challenging. No one had been able to prove that theorem for several days. Then the student who sat next to me, whose name was Randy, raised his hand and said he could prove it. He went to the board and successfully proved it as I watched. I had not even attempted to prove that theorem. But I remember saying to myself, "I could have done that." At that moment I realized that I should actually prove the theorems on my own.

With that change in perspective, I enjoyed the great pleasure of proving all the delightfully difficult theorems for the rest of the year. The challenges were like a jar of delicious candy to me. Under that method of instruction, I learned the material in a far deeper way than I had ever learned any knowledge before. At the conclusion of the year, and to this day, I could easily take out a blank piece of paper and write down the entire content of the course, including the statements and proofs of all the theorems.

One goal of education is to transform students from consumers of knowledge into producers of knowledge. It is an exhilarating transformation. Teaching the joy of thinking can encourage students to become the independent, creative thinkers with whom we would prefer our world be populated.

> Teaching the joy of thinking can encourage students to become the independent, creative thinkers with whom we would prefer our world be populated.

MICHAEL STARBIRD

*What's the difference between
a teacher and a mentor?*

"I'M LOOKING THROUGH YOU"
(TO BUILD RESISTANCE
TO MANIPULATION)

THE BEATLES SONG "I'm Looking Through You" offers some useful lines for teachers. I know that for first-year composition students, dissertation writers, and students at every level in between, I've quoted the line "The words aren't clear." But that song is certainly a poor teaching manual. We've been taught to engage students. Make eye contact. Don't look through them. Still, there is a fundamental truth to the perception of teaching as a "looking-through" experience. Too often we get caught up in the moment of teaching. Immediate or short-term goals become blinders that prevent us from seeing opportunities to help students resist manipulation after they graduate.

In my first year of teaching, I'm sure my blinders were quite thick. I was hired as an assistant professor of English, but my PhD was in American studies. I was determined to prove to my colleagues that I could teach first-year composition. I focused on developing specific skills: how to write a topic sentence, how to outline, and how to appeal to an audience. Besides teaching writing skills for college courses, I hope my approach helped some of the students after they graduated in careers that involved writing.

But a question from one student in a composition class a couple of years later taught me how limited my vision was. She was a thirty-six-year-old grandmother and the smartest student in the class. The assignment was to imagine a transformed Arlington, Texas—a utopian Arlington. She came up to me as others were writing and whispered, "What if I think Arlington is utopia?" Students who overheard her snickered. But their ideas (which included more parking spaces) suggested that they also had trouble thinking beyond the present. Our educational system wasn't doing a very good job of enabling students to define what they wanted in the future. Therefore, ad campaigns, talk-show hosts, charlatan religious leaders, and politicians, who all thrive on telling people what they should desire, could manipulate these students.

My most elaborate response to this problem was a "Build Your Own Utopia" course, inspired by a team-based, problem-solving pedagogy—known as Guided Design—that was designed by engineers at West Virginia University. For example, one of the problems challenges students to develop a plan to create one "ideal" individual. The problem solving, which proceeds through a series of instructions and feedback, involves many practical and ethical issues, including defining what students mean by ideal and defining the human and environmental conditions related to this concept. This process invites students to consider what each of them desires to be as an individual.

There are some courses that lend themselves more obviously than others to this type of "looking-through" pedagogy—for instance, engineering and science classes in sustainability. But "looking through" can be a part of almost any course if, before presenting each assignment, a teacher asks herself, "How will this assignment impact the students' abilities to define what they want and thus render them less likely to be the victims of future manipulators who want to impose their desires on them?" The question can be used in the study of a historical era by provoking students to ask if they want a repetition of the circumstances in that time period, in a lab experiment by highlighting the tensions between the desired results and the temptation to manipulate evidence, in a studio art project by speculating about how the project might shape how people want to define beauty or ugliness, and in many other types of courses. If this kind of looking through helps students think beyond desires for more parking lots and helps build resistance to unethical manipulators, then we will certainly have given them a good education.

KENNETH ROEMER

*Students will rise to the level of
your expectations; set them high.*

BE CAREFUL—
THEY ARE SENSITIVE BEINGS

PROFESSORS HAVE MANY STUDENTS each semester. We get busy; we get careless. Students usually have only four or five professors each term. They want you to notice and like them. What you say, or don't say, or telegraph with a look can loom much larger in their lives than you may expect.

> They want you to notice and like them.

And then there is this thing called *stereotype vulnerability*. Apparently for some students, the normal stress of learning new things can trigger reminders of negative stereotypes, such as "Women aren't as good at math as men" or "Those who study the humanities are wasting their time." Students can begin to feel judged (or to negatively judge themselves) even when their professor has said or done nothing that is in any way judgmental. Once a student starts to think a professor is unsympathetic to his identity group, in most cases he will shut down, often silently, giving the professor no indication of what has happened. It is mighty hard to save such a situation. So be careful. Students are sensitive beings.

CATHERINE ROSS

Never just read your syllabus on the first day. Teach something!

YOUR CLASS IS NOT THEIR LIFE

TEACHING IS LIKE A GAS; it takes up all available space. Boy, this is true. Especially when we first start teaching. We get so excited about the subject matter and dedicate lots of time to figuring out how to teach it and make sure the students learn it, and then to seeing whether or not they do.

> Teaching is like a gas;
> it takes up all available space.

But we might be a little shocked, maybe even a little hurt, when we later learn that our students don't share the same enthusiasm for our class that we do—that to them learning in our class is not a gas, not exactly. That realization usually comes pretty hard for first-time teachers. This often happens around October or November. By this point, new teachers have put an immense amount of time into a class and have evaluated a couple of major projects. These enthusiastic instructors say things like "My students clearly aren't trying because I'm helping them as much as I can. Why won't they just spend the time to do it well?"

Of course, there are a number of students who are able and willing to put in the extra time to be successful. Or maybe they just *love* your class. There may be quite a few others, however, who are also working, taking care of a family member, or just aren't that interested (gasp!) in what you are teaching. Realizing this sooner rather than later helps us to adjust our perspective. Rather than simplifying the course or reducing the number of projects, we might rethink the way we approach the course content and assignments. Maybe there are ways to workshop ideas or projects in class to give students a running start. Maybe boring assignments can be given a facelift by connecting them to current events in the discipline. Maybe we have to come to grips with the fact that for some students, passing this class with a C is just fine on balance with working twenty-five hours a week and sharing home responsibilities with their younger siblings. Does this mean they are worse students than those who invest more time? Of course not. It simply means they have a life, and my class isn't the most important thing in it. I can live with that!

BETH BRUNK-CHAVEZ

The best teaching encourages students to ask more questions.

GIVE THANKS . . .
AND PRIME THE PUMP

THE LAST ITEM on the student card described earlier, the name of a teacher who has been a valuable influence (see "Connections" on page 52), offers an opportunity to solidify the relationship with a student while reaching out to dedicated, effective teachers in our vast network of high schools in Texas and in the world beyond. Again, it is the pervasive technology at our fingertips that brings this connection within reach.

With the name of the teacher and high school already in hand, a quick web search will usually produce a mailing address. Then, working from a thoughtfully prepared model, a letter can be individually crafted that tells how the teacher was singled out for her influence and support during the student's precollege years. It has been my experience that the letter has multiple positive consequences. Although it is not directly from the student, it does convey a message that is too infrequently expressed—that the student values the contribution the teacher has made during an important time of

> The student values the contribution the teacher has made during an important time of growth and development.

growth and development. For the teacher, the letter often comes at the end of a semester when fatigue may be raising doubts about whether all the hard work is appreciated. The letter also has the benefit of surprise, and it establishes a link between the high school and the university.

Of course this project is not entirely altruistic. In fact, I make it clear in the letter that we thrive on the quality of our students and that we hope to see more well-prepared prospects coming to our campus in the future.

JAMES VICK

Q: If students are customers, and if the customer is always right, then what's the point of attempting to educate them?

A: —

CONCLUDING THOUGHTS

FIRST THINGS FIRST

I AM NOT USUALLY well enough organized to prioritize efficiently. I just fight little battles as they come at me. Stephen Covey observed that "most of us spend too much time on what is urgent and not enough time on what is important," and I routinely fall victim to this tendency. There is one exception, however, to this general ineptitude on my part—I always remember to put my teaching first.

Like others in academia, I have research obligations, administrative responsibilities, and other tasks that I cannot shirk. But in the academic realm of my life I have learned to put first things first. And for me, teaching comes first.

Late every afternoon, I make a list of the things that I hope to do the following day. Some must get done. I would be delighted if I got to some of the others. Whenever items related to class preparation are on the list, as they almost always are, they get my attention first. This emphasis is not necessarily consistent with the official reward structure at my school. Still, it works for me. I like research and writing. I truly do. But my vision

> Doris Lessing had it right when she said, "It is the mark of great people to treat trifles as trifles and important matters as important."

of myself as a college professor features most prominently my role as a classroom teacher. Therefore, teaching always comes first among my professional responsibilities. Doris Lessing had it right when she said, "It is the mark of great people to treat trifles as trifles and important matters as important."

ROBERT PRENTICE

Who was the very best teacher you ever had? What made him or her so impressive? How are you emulating such teaching greatness?

TEACHING BEYOND THE CLASSROOM

SOME OF THE MOST IMPORTANT TEACHING takes place beyond the classroom. I have often thought of teaching and learning as the concentric, ever-widening circles that result from a pebble thrown in the calm water of a lake—some rings clearly visible, others barely perceptible. Some of these imperceptible, ever-widening circles, I am convinced, are located outside the classroom. For instance, I take the time to mentor especially strong students by talking to them about graduate school and also by introducing them to the world of academic publishing. On numerous occasions, I have assisted students in publishing their work even while they were pursuing an MA, something my professors never did! At first, I help them discover journals that would potentially be interested in their work and have them read several articles to understand the sophistication and style of the contributors and the type of

> Some of the most important teaching takes place beyond the classroom. I have often thought of teaching and learning as the concentric, ever-widening circles that result from a pebble thrown in the calm water of a lake—some rings clearly visible, others barely perceptible.

audience these journals try to reach. Then I go over several drafts of their papers until they are ready for submission. I don't know who is more excited when that paper is accepted for publication—me or the student. I recently got a message on Facebook from a student who passed her comprehensives in May and got a tenure-track job for the fall. She wrote, "People congratulate me on completing my PhD but they don't know that I could not have done it without you." I mentored this student through the MA program and helped her publish two articles. In the second year she was pursuing her MA, and while I was serving as the chair of my department, I decided to do something very unusual. I babysat for her in the evening to enable her to attend one of her MA classes because she could not find a babysitter and was a single parent.

Sometimes I identify gaps in students' knowledge or writing and form groups to address their needs. I often have them work on each other's papers to improve their own style and grammar. Taking students on field trips is yet another way to expand their knowledge and have them better understand the connection between the academic and the "real" world. In my case, I take students to galleries to see paintings we have discussed in class. I often tell them that no matter how good an art historian is, she cannot possibly describe the feeling they will experience while standing in front of a painting. And that feeling is one of numerous discoveries they make in art galleries. Last year, I collaborated with an art professor and taught a Maymester course that included a trip to London and Paris. This trip was a life-changing experience for most of the students. Next year I am taking them to southern France and Italy.

Activities beyond the classroom make enormous demands on our time, already heavily taxed by our teaching, writing, and service and administrative responsibilities. But students' grateful responses to this additional work can be the most gratifying rewards we receive in our academic careers.

SOPHIA ANDRES

You are what you teach.

WHAT'S YOUR LEGACY?

THOSE FAMILIAR WITH Stephen Covey's work can readily recite the first habit of the highly effective person: "Begin with the end in mind." Those unfamiliar with the Coveysphere have certainly heard—and offered—similar aphorisms in the contexts of coaching, advising, and mentoring. What's important to appreciate about Covey's take on "the end" is that he's not talking about "end" as "goal" but as "aftereffect" or even "afterlife." Through this lens, the successful teacher's efforts to "begin with the end in mind" aren't so much about establishing clear student learning outcomes or placing a course into the larger curricular context (both important *goals*), but more about considering the effect that he will have on students beyond the course

> Years from now, what will students remember about me as a teacher?

(the long-term *impact*). He might ask himself, "Years from now, what will students remember about me as a teacher?"

One useful way of framing your desired teaching legacy might be found in your institution's end-of-term student survey: what kind of feedback will be solicited about your instruction? Will students tell you that you communicated clearly or not? Will they let you know that you weren't as available as you thought you were? Will they praise your ability to engage them in meaningful ways? I'll be the first to admit that course evaluations of this sort aren't the be-all and end-all to assess one's teaching (and they should not be), but I'll also point out two things about such surveys. First, they're not going away anytime soon, so we ought to take them seriously. Second, they're not (all) inherently bad. In fact, the items presented in a reasonably designed end-of-term survey can serve as a useful template.

Note that I'm not talking about the *data* generated by such surveys. There's ample evidence to suggest that how students rate professors can be influenced by any number of factors, many of which can't be controlled and others of which can be manipulated by easy As and in-class snacks. What's at play are the attributes to which such surveys point, attributes often associated with the very best teachers.

So try this exercise. With your local survey in hand, go through each item and rate the two or three very best teachers you ever had, the ones you remember with great fondness and admiration for their ability to inspire students to learn. How did they do? Now ask the same questions of yourself, not only in the abstract, but—if you're diligent— at the end of each week. How did you do when it came to communicating clearly? Establishing expectations? Engaging students' minds? Being accessible? Finally, project yourself into the future. When you are gone, what will your former students have to say about your teaching? If you, like Ebenezer Scrooge, don't like what the third ghost has to offer, change. Today.

DAVID SILVA

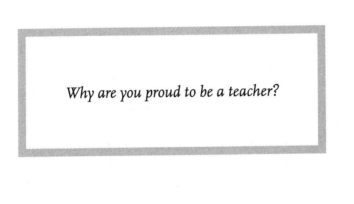

Why are you proud to be a teacher?

FINISHING WELL

ADVANCING AGE BRINGS with it a host of new challenges, from hearing loss to fading short-term memory. These hardships may be accompanied by the emergence of some disease or chronic condition that adds yet another dimension to the daily academic struggle. But we are fortunate to be in a profession that may allow us to continue to be productive in the classroom well beyond the age at which others have seen their careers end. I saw this with my mother and father, both teachers who loved their disciplines and their students.

My own personal challenge has come from a diagnosis of Parkinson's disease six years ago. The slow progression of this illness has allowed me to continue my work and to gradually move toward retirement. In doing so, I have had time to reflect on the experience, and this reflection, as expressed in the following poem, has helped me deal with the concluding chapter of my journey.

> It's hard, when life has brought acclaim,
> When heights were mine to climb,
> To feel I'm lifted from the game
> While I'm still in my prime.

I dream of building once again
A world where students thrive.
Relationships, careers begin,
And futures come alive.

I long once more to throw a pass
Or turn a double play,
Instead of hearing others ask,
"How do you feel today?"

As other doors are slowly closed,
Putting dreams beyond my reach,
I walk the path my parents chose.
I pass the torch, I teach.

JAMES VICK

CONTRIBUTORS

SOPHIA ANDRES is Kathlyn Cosper Dunagan Professor in the Humanities at the University of Texas of the Permian Basin, where she teaches Victorian and modern British fiction and art. Her *Pre-Raphaelite Art of the Victorian Novel* received the Book of the Year Award from the South Central Modern Language Association. Currently she is working on two books, *Poetry in Painting* and *Pre-Raphaelite Ghosts in the Modern Novel*.

BETH BRUNK-CHAVEZ is an associate professor of rhetoric and writing studies at the University of Texas at El Paso, where she is also the senior associate dean of Extended University. She was formerly the director of the First-Year Composition program, which won the Conference on Composition and Communication Writing Program of Excellence Award in 2012. Her research interests are in online education, writing with technology, and writing program administration.

MARY LYNN CROW is a licensed psychologist, professor of education, Piper Professor of Texas, and director of the counseling program at the University of Texas at Arlington. She founded the first faculty instructional development center in the University of Texas System, and was the first executive director of the Professional and Organizational Development Network in Higher Education. She is a former public school teacher, counselor, and Romper Room Teacher on the Romper Room International Television Kindergarten.

JOHN DALY is Liddell Carter Professor in the College of Communication, Texas Commerce Bancshares Professor in the McCombs School of Business, and Distinguished Teaching Professor at the University of Texas at Austin. He has won every campuswide undergraduate teaching award at the university. A fellow of both the National Communication Association and International Communication Association, he has also authored more than a hundred scholarly articles and nine books.

PATRICK DAVIS is Eckerd Centennial Professor in pharmacy and currently serves as senior associate dean for Academic Affairs for the College of Pharmacy at the University of Texas at Austin. He completed his BS and PhD at the University of Iowa, and has taught at the University of Texas for thirty-five years. His research focuses on the impact of educational technology on student learning, and his teaching largely addresses infectious diseases.

NEIL GRAY serves as professor and chair of the Department of Chemistry and Biochemistry at the University of Texas at Tyler, and is also co-director for the UTeach program there. He is a recipient of the Piper Professorship for Excellence in Teaching, the Chancellor's Council Outstanding Teaching Award, and the University of Texas System Board of Regents' Outstanding Teaching Award. His research interests are in the areas of nanoparticles, polymer surface modification, medicinal chemistry, and chemical education.

JOHN HADJIMARCOU is professor of marketing at the University of Texas at El Paso and fellow in the University of Texas System Academy of Distinguished Teachers. John is passionate about creative simplicity in teaching. He is also a strong advocate of faculty development programs for academic career success.

BRENT IVERSON, the Warren J. and Viola Mae Raymer Professor of Chemistry, is currently serving as dean of the School of Undergraduate Studies at the University of Texas of Austin. His research career spans the interface of chemistry and biology, and he is best known for developing a cure for late-stage anthrax infection. He is the author of a popular textbook and has won numerous awards while teaching large organic chemistry classes for premedical students.

ROBERT PRENTICE is the Ed & Molly Smith Professor of Business Law at the McCombs School of Business at the University of Texas at Austin. He is currently chair of the Department of Business, Government & Society; faculty director of the Business Honors Program; and faculty director of the Ethics Unwrapped video project. He is a member of the inaugural class of the University of Texas at Austin Academy of Distinguished Teachers and the University of Texas System Academy of Distinguished Teachers, and a winner of the University of Texas System Board of Regents' Outstanding Teaching Award.

KENNETH ROEMER is a Piper Professor, Distinguished Teaching Professor, Distinguished Scholar Professor, National Endowment for the Humanities grantee, and Pulitzer Prize nominee at the University of Texas at Arlington. He has guest-lectured at Harvard University and in twelve countries. His eight books focus on Native American and utopian literature.

CATHERINE ROSS teaches British literature, rhetoric, and composition at the University of Texas at Tyler. She is working on a book, *British Learning, 1760–1840*, which endeavors to explain the British Romantics' remarkable productivity and unique literary contributions by exploring how they were educated.

JOHN SIBERT is currently an associate professor of chemistry at the University of Texas at Dallas. His research interests are in molecular architecture—designing and building new molecules for applications that span from medicine to environmental science to advanced new materials. He is an author, inventor, and award-winning teacher with an educational emphasis on engaging learners in innovative methods centered around curiosity and discovery.

DAVID J. SILVA has served as professor of linguistics, Distinguished Teaching Professor, and Vice Provost for Faculty Affairs at the University of Texas at Arlington. His linguistic research addresses topics in phonetic and phonological variation in languages as diverse as Portuguese, Korean, Dinka, and English. He currently serves as Provost and Academic Vice President at Salem State University, Salem, Massachusetts.

MICHAEL STARBIRD is a University Distinguished Teaching Professor of Mathematics at the University of Texas at Austin, where he directs the Inquiry Based Learning project. He has received numerous national, statewide, and campus teaching awards, and has produced DVD courses for The Teaching Company in The Great Courses series. He is an author or coauthor of a number of popular books, including *The 5 Elements of Effective Thinking*, which is published by Princeton University Press.

JAMES VICK is Ashbel Smith Professor and Distinguished Teaching Professor of Mathematics at the University of Texas at Austin. In addition to his teaching and research, he has served as associate dean of natural sciences, vice president for student affairs, and faculty athletic representative.

MICHAEL WEBBER is deputy director of the Energy Institute, co-director of the Clean Energy Incubator, Josey Centennial Fellow in Energy Resources, and associate professor of mechanical engineering at the University of Texas at Austin, where he trains the next generation of energy leaders and conducts research on energy and environmental topics. He is the author of *Energy101*, a digital guide to energy, and has gained public attention for national syndication of his television special "Energy at the Movies" on PBS.